I0392618

MOUNTS 2
Coloring book

AUTHOR AND ILLUSTRATOR
OLGA GOLOVESHKINA

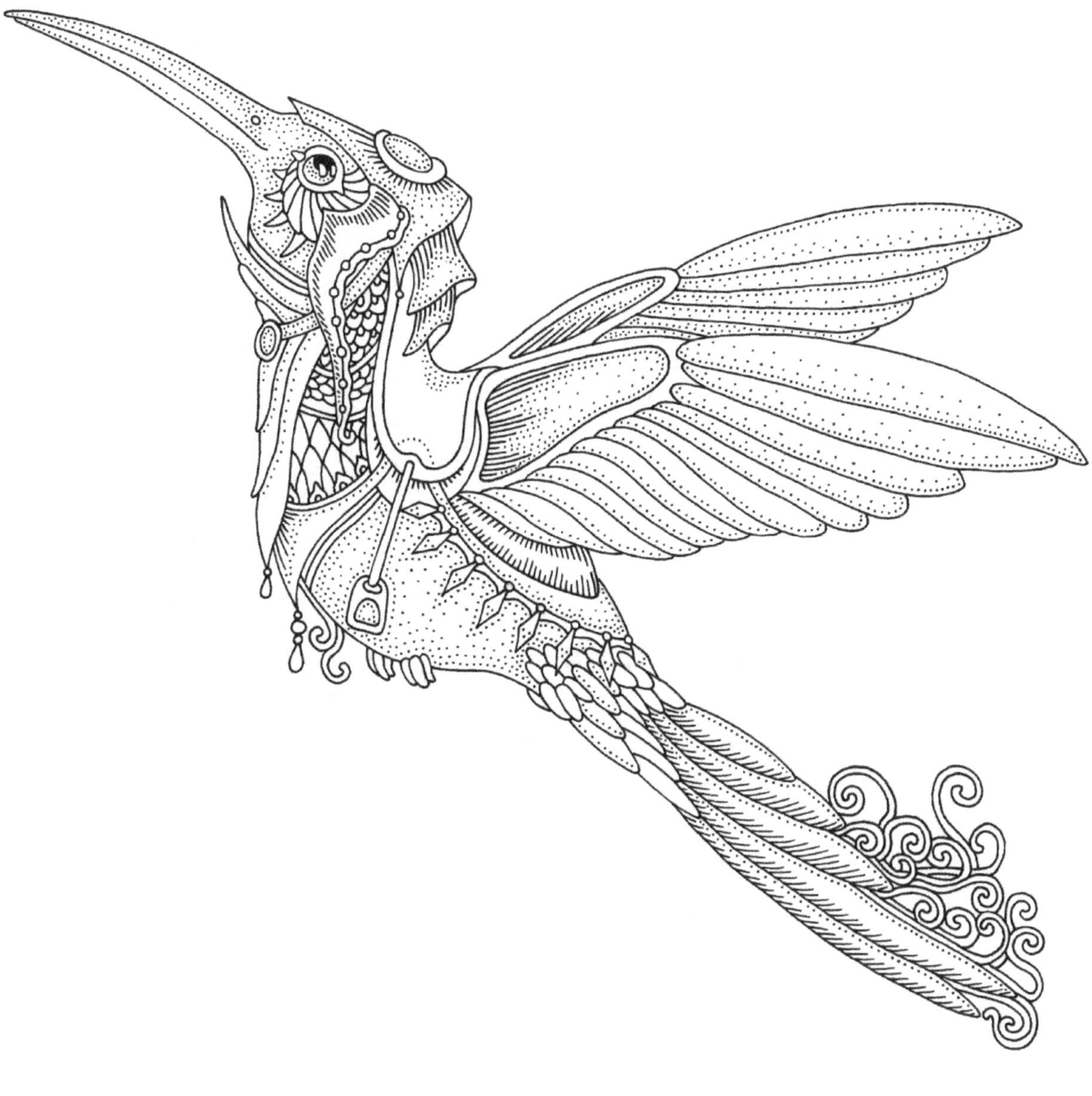

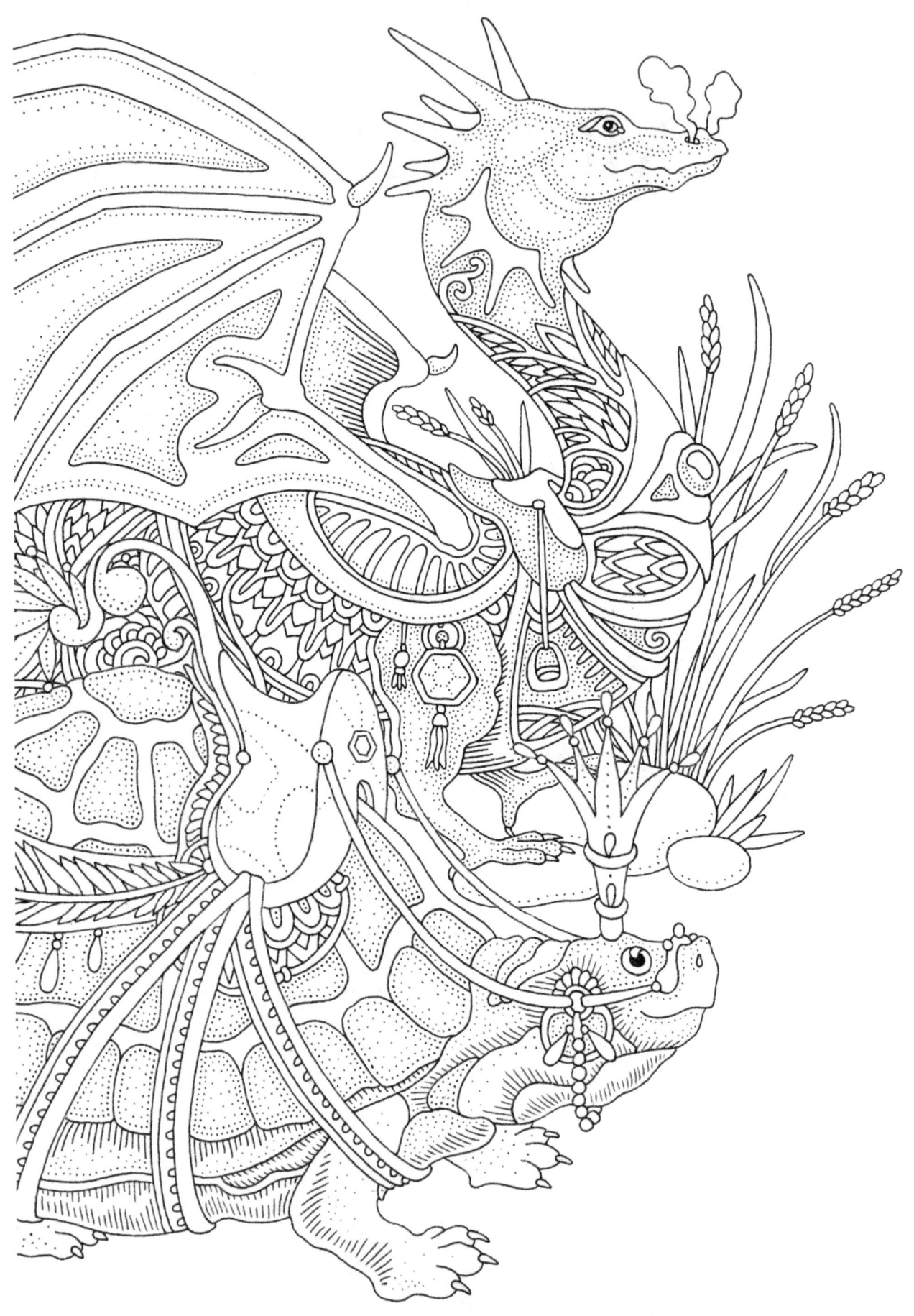

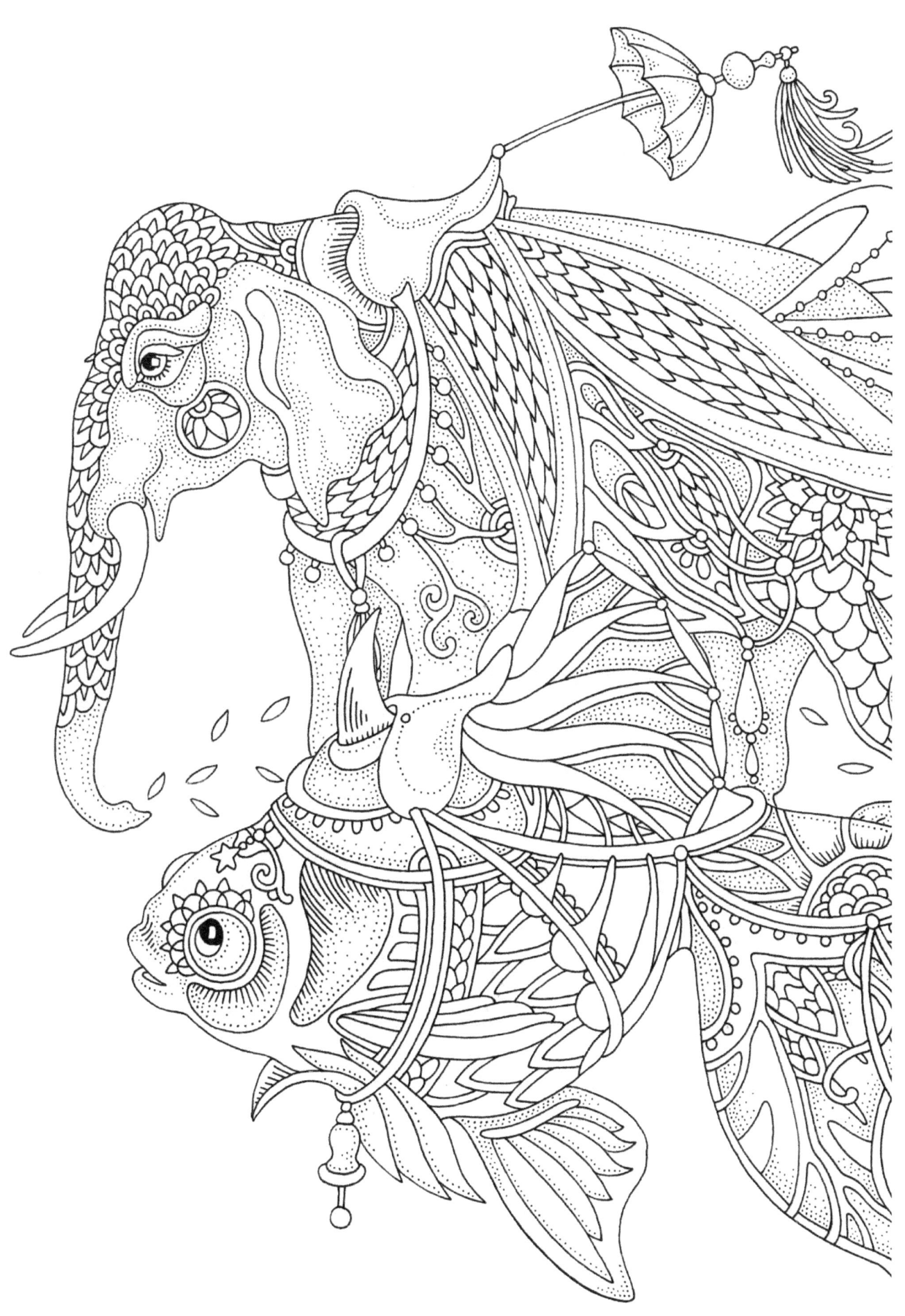

ISBN: 1537365495
ISBN-13: 9781537365497

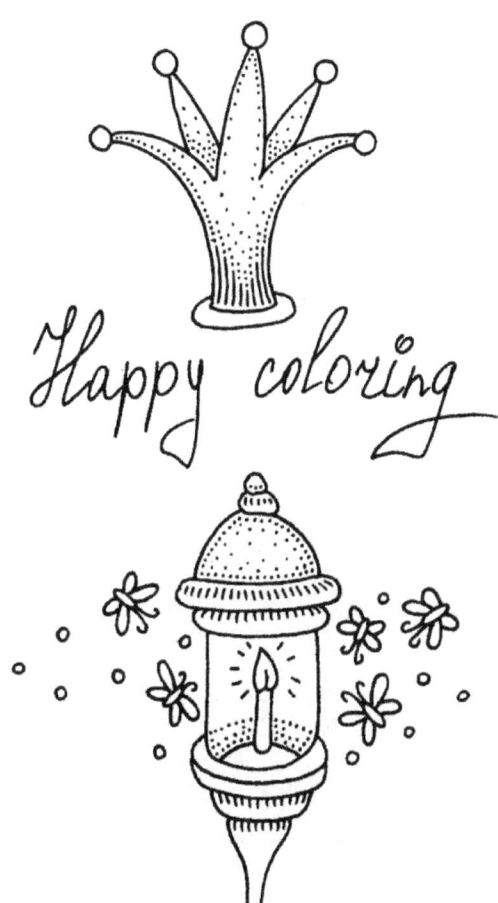

Happy coloring

Thank you for choosing
my coloring book!

Olya :)

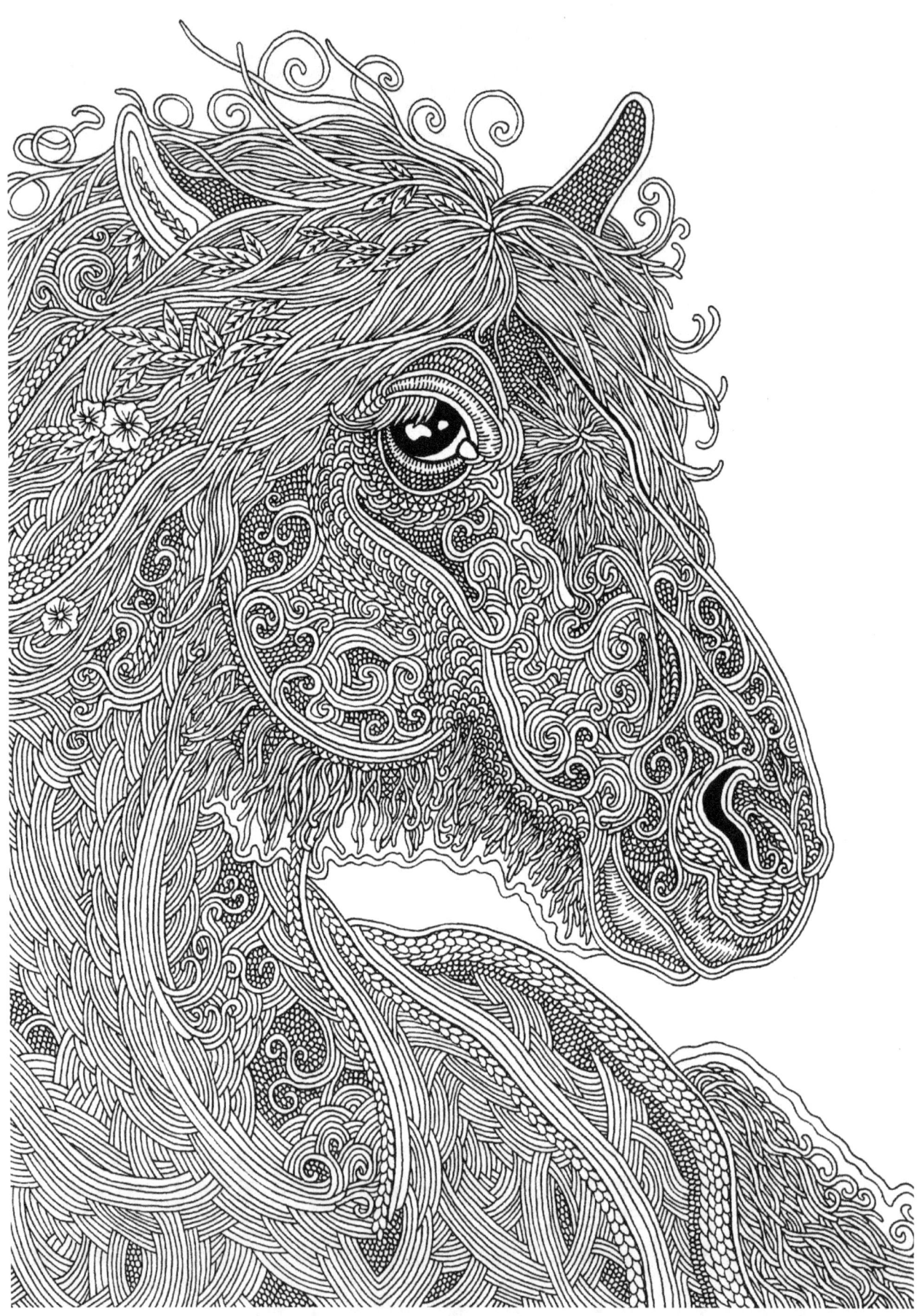

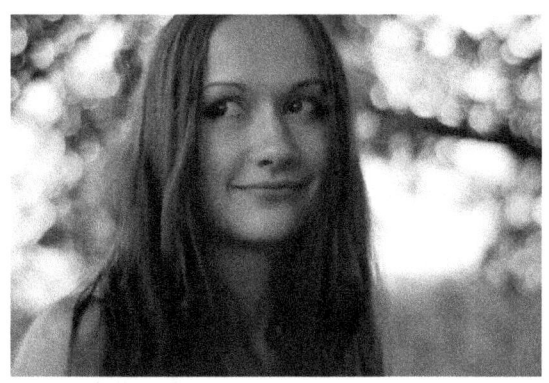

ABOUT THE AUTHOR

Olga Goloveshkina is a freelance artist and illustrator
based in Moscow, Russia.
She graduated from the Institute of Busines and Design.
Olga specializes in black ink doodles.
She is an author and illustrator coloring books for adults
"The wind carries flowers"/"Veter unosit tsvety" (in Russian),
"Fox travel: Coloring book" and "Mounts: Coloring book" (in English).

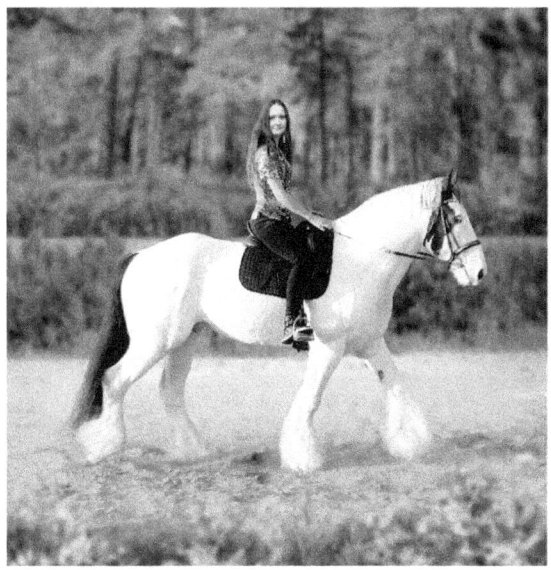

Author page on Amazon:
amazon.com/author/olgagoloveshkina
Site: http://olyagoloveshkina.jimdo.com
Instagram:
@olyahitrayapanda
@olyagoloveshkina

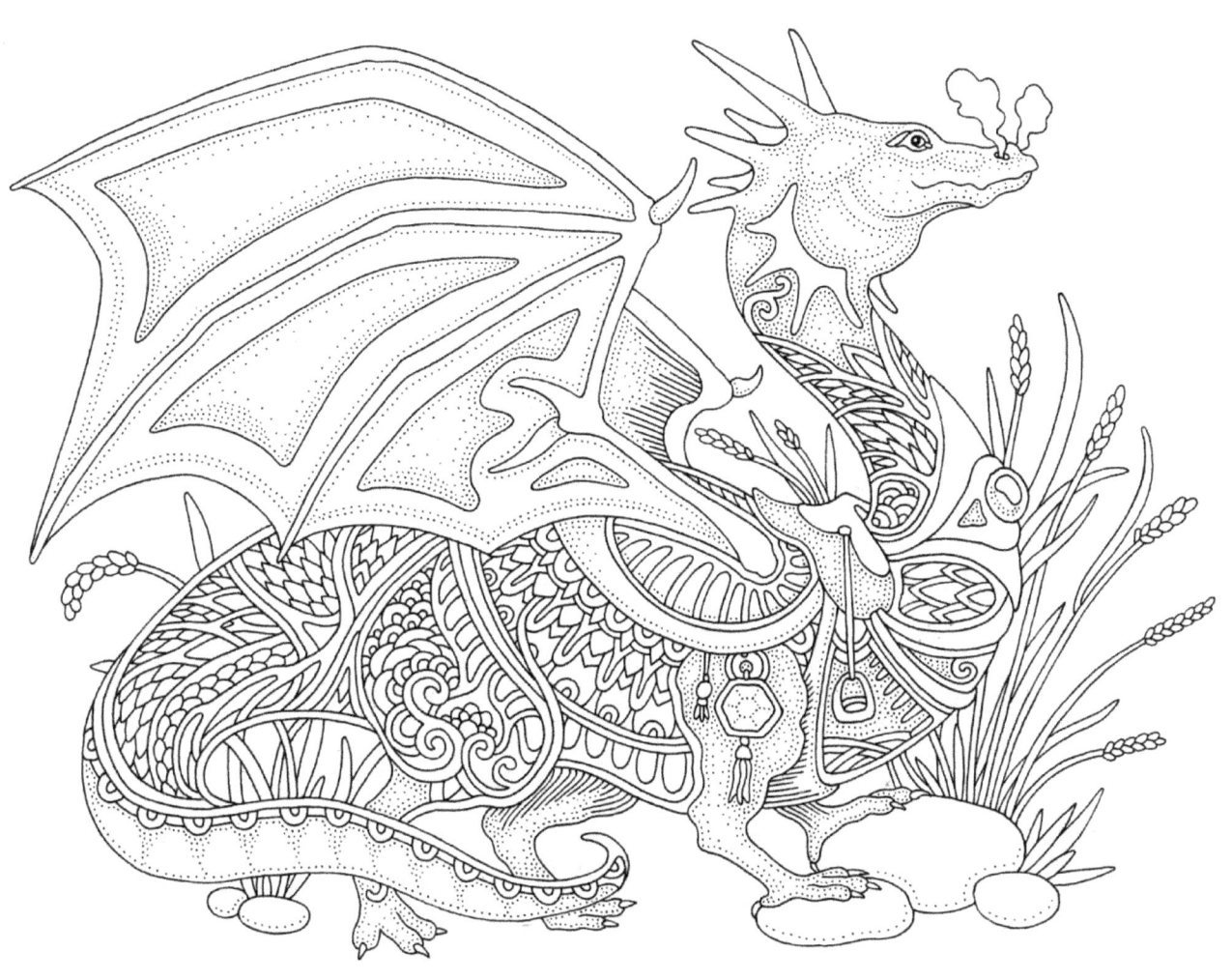

This book belongs to

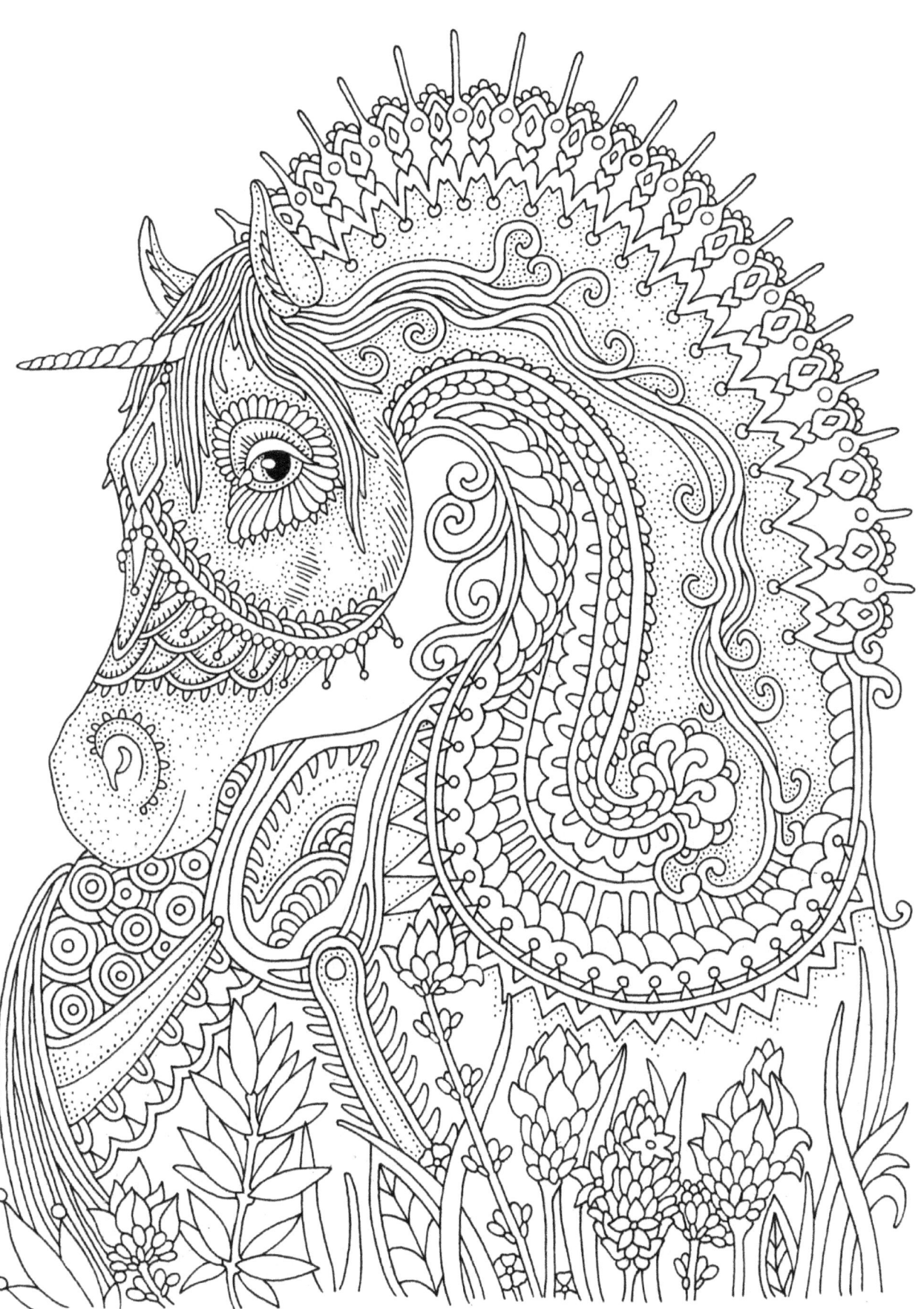

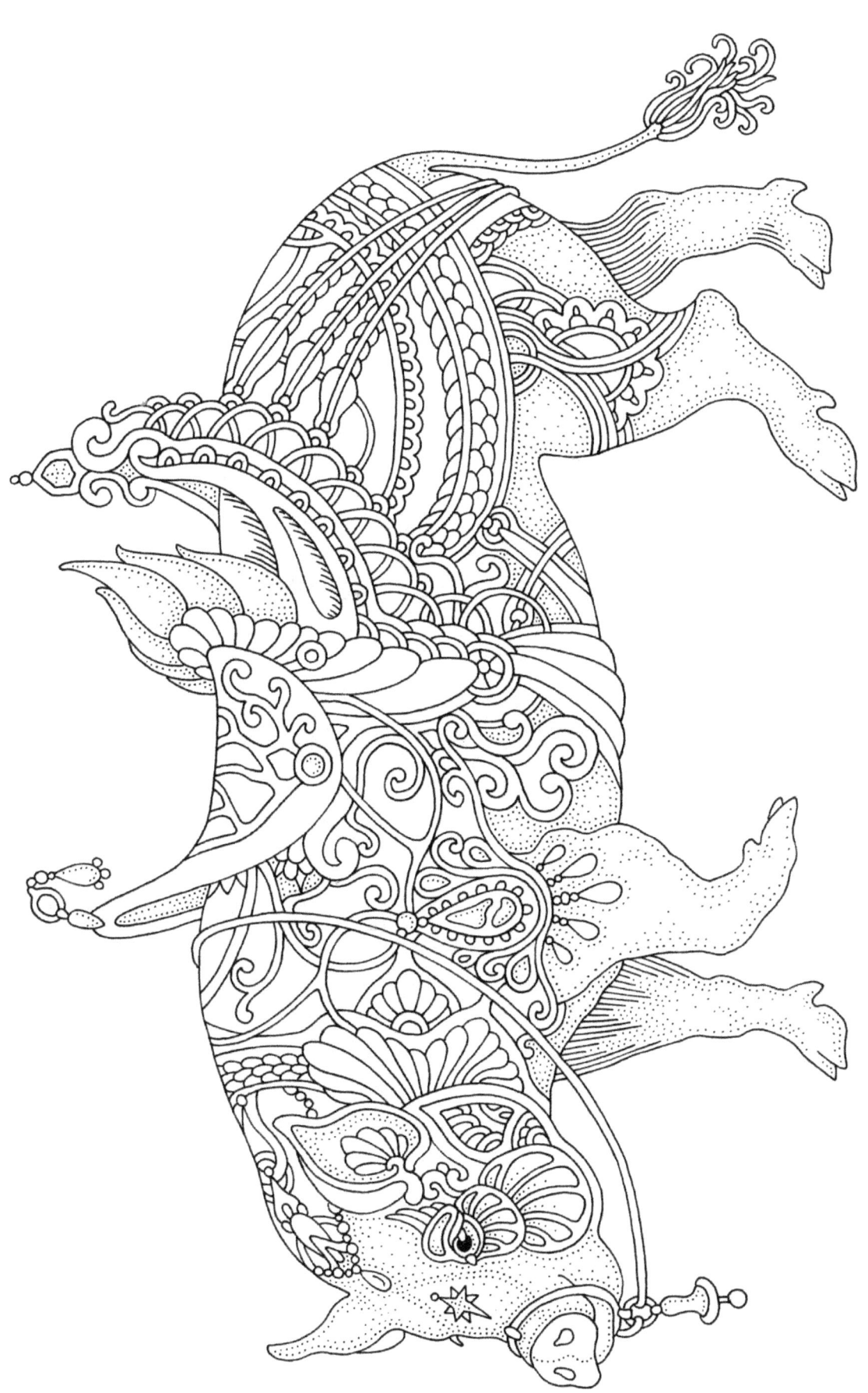

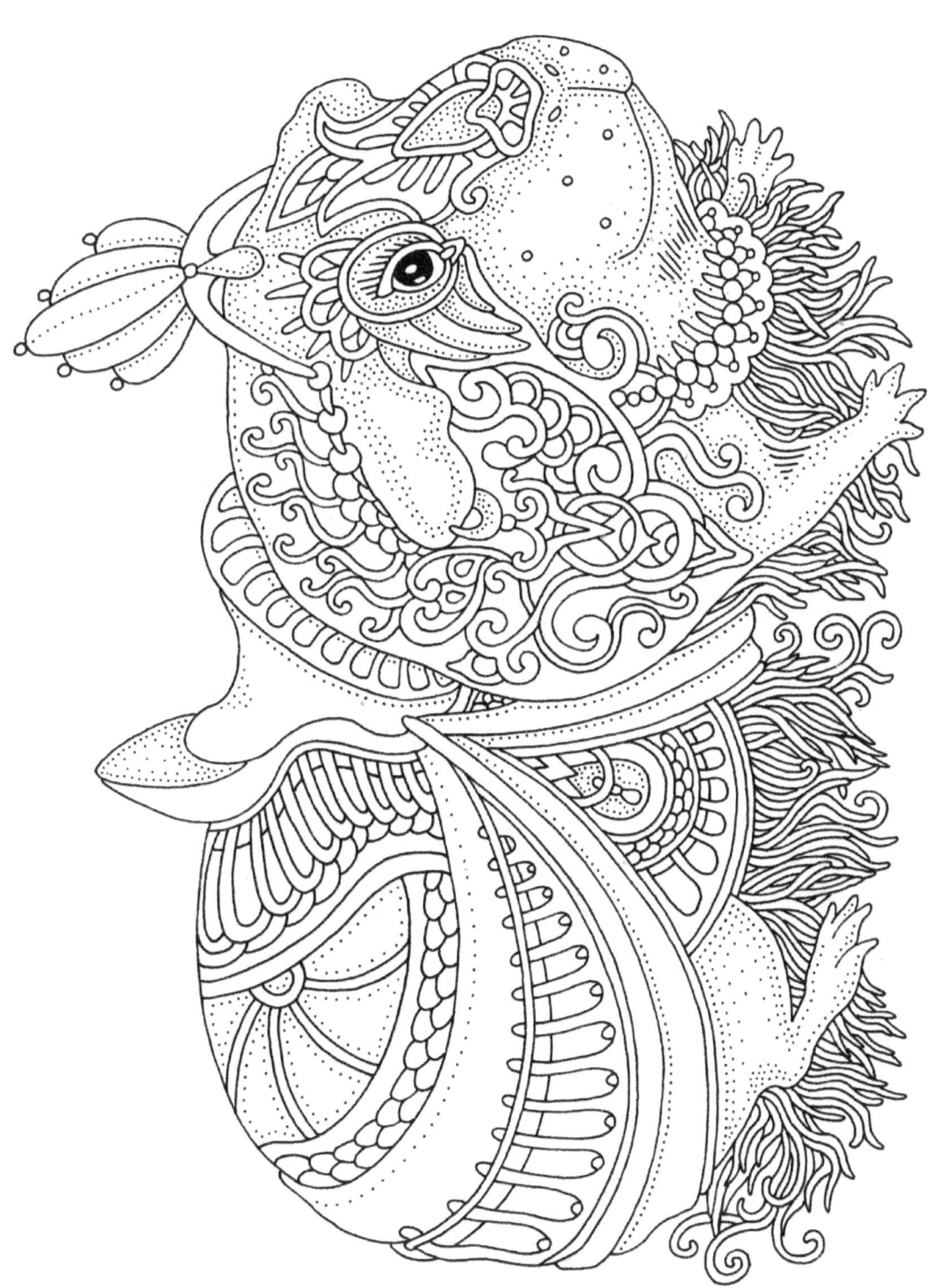

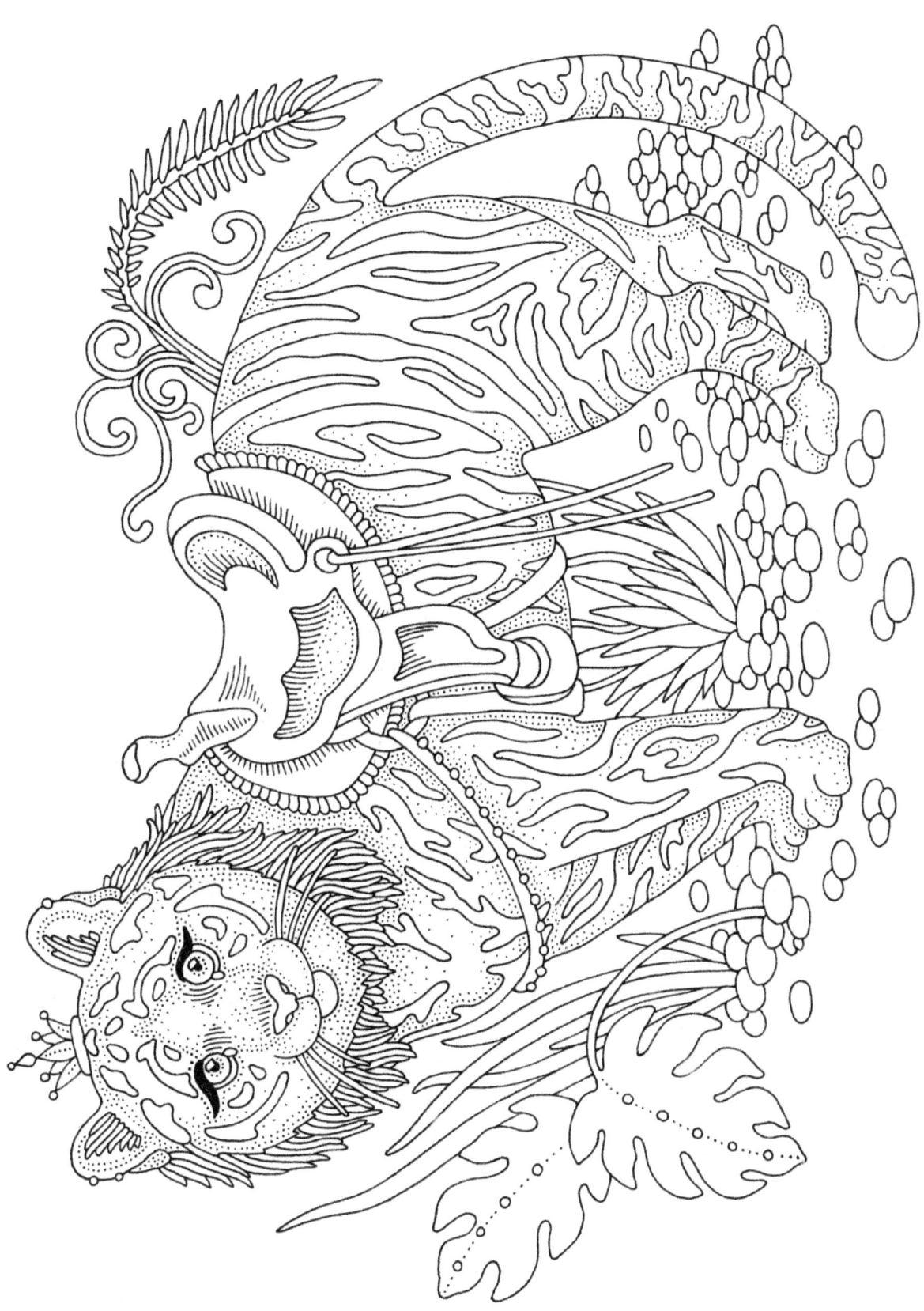

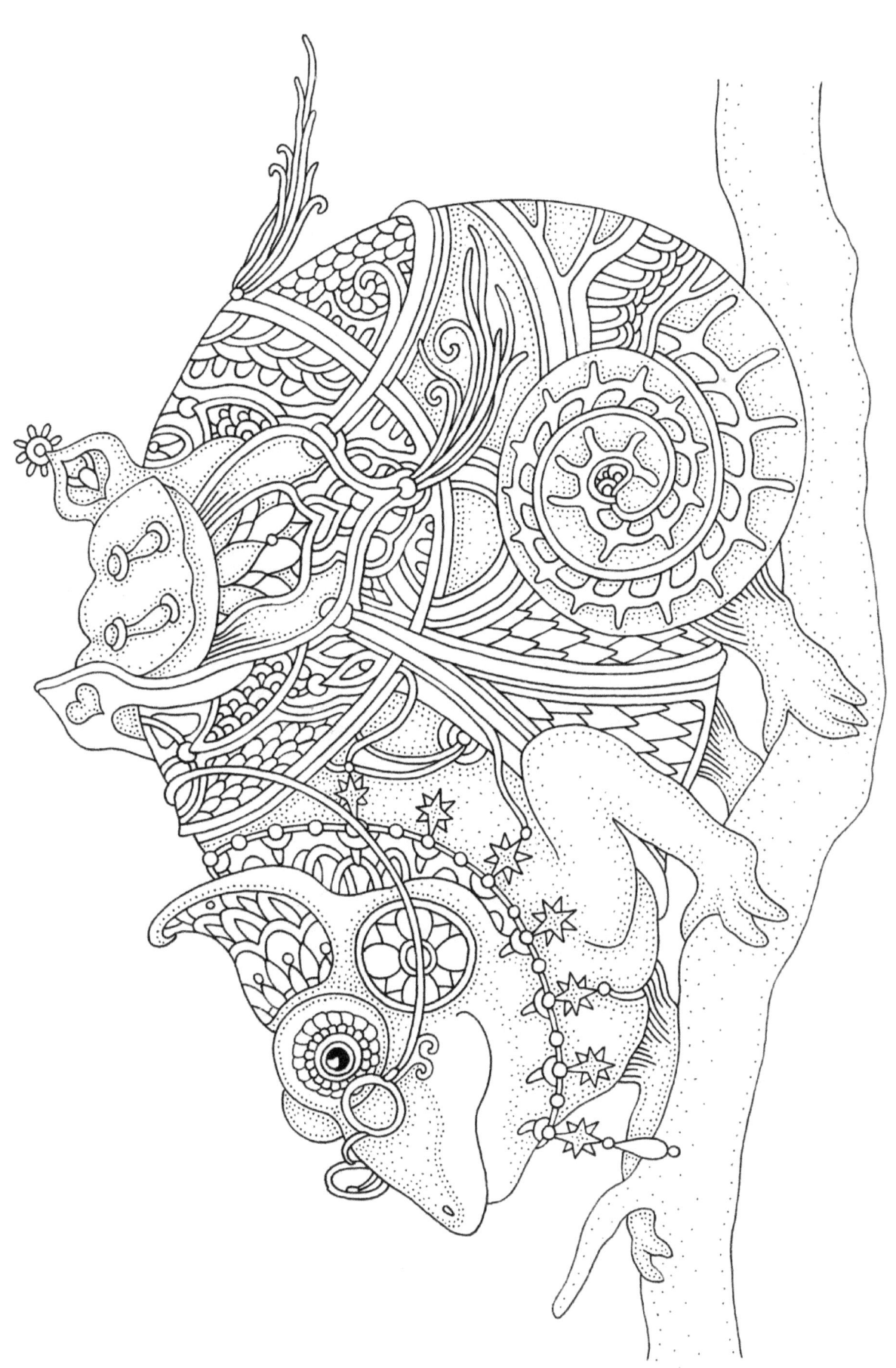

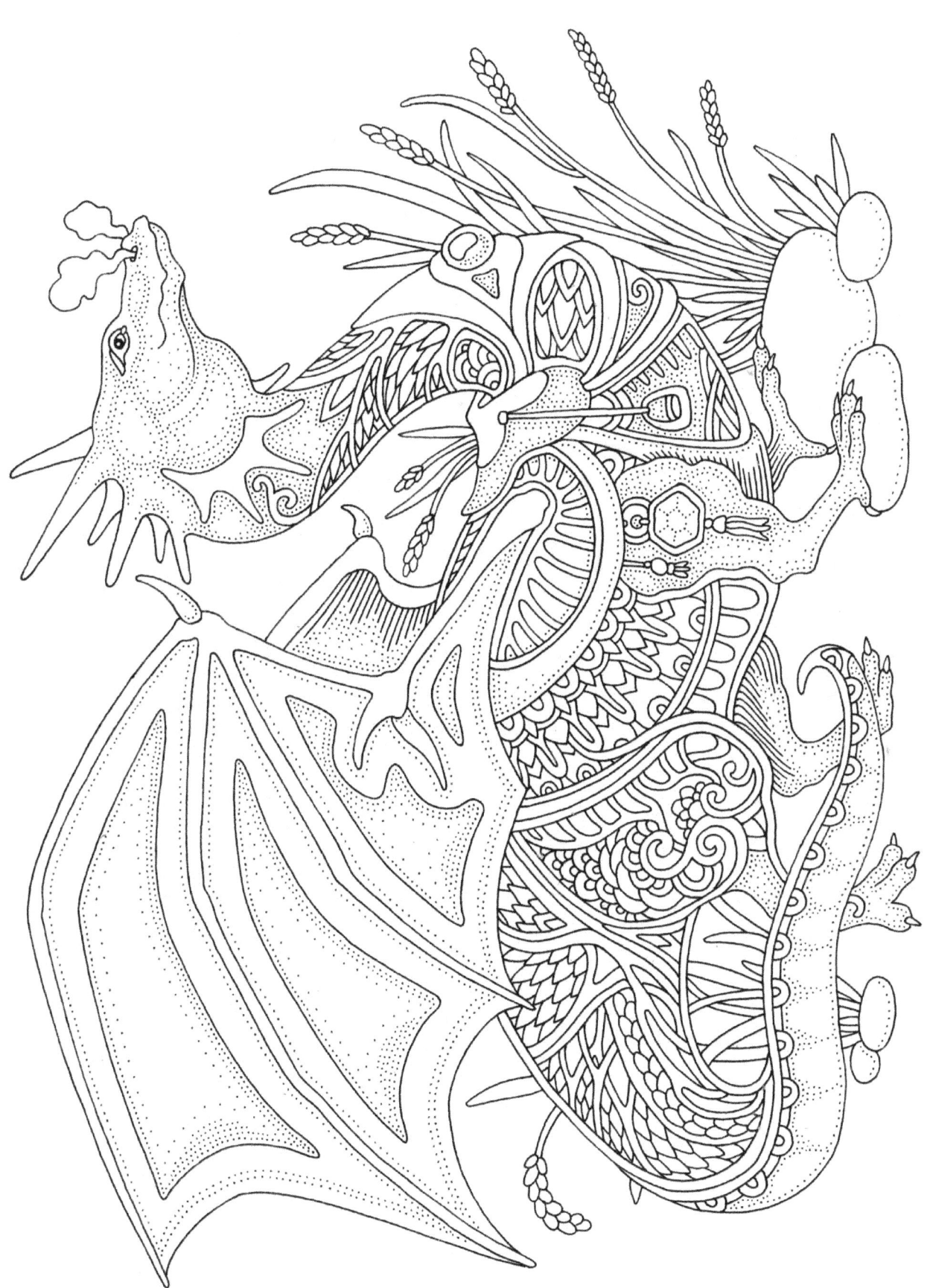

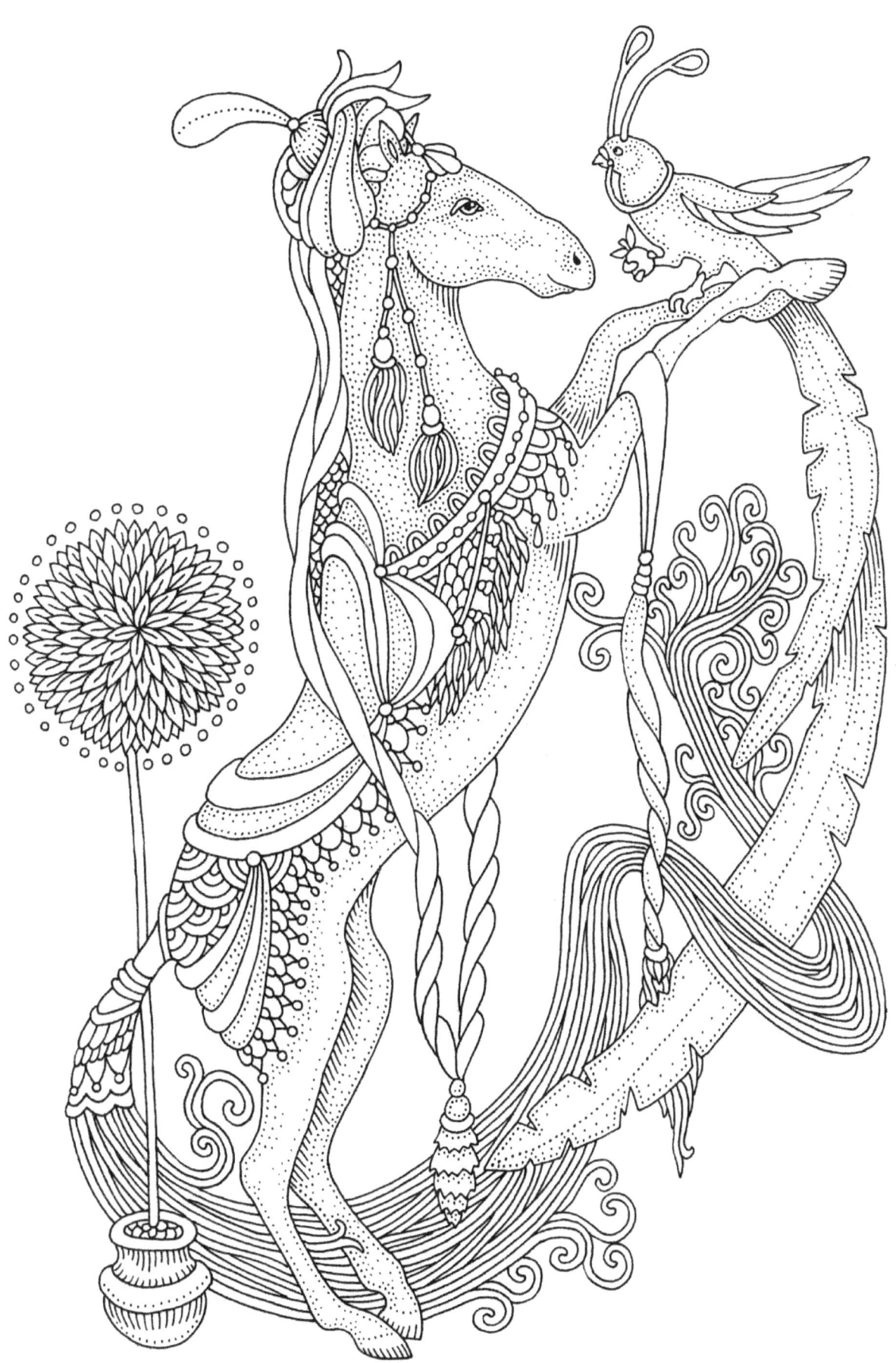

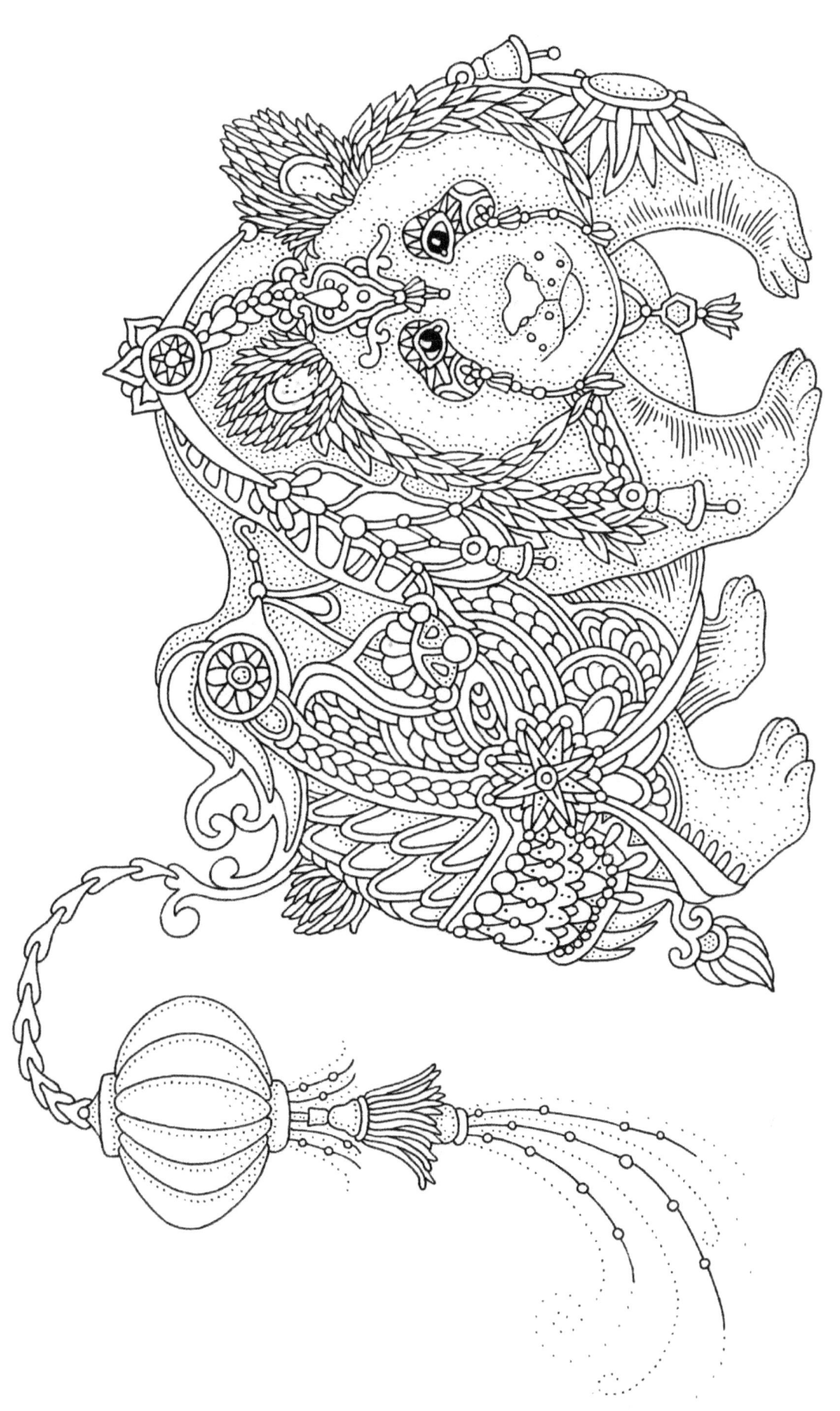

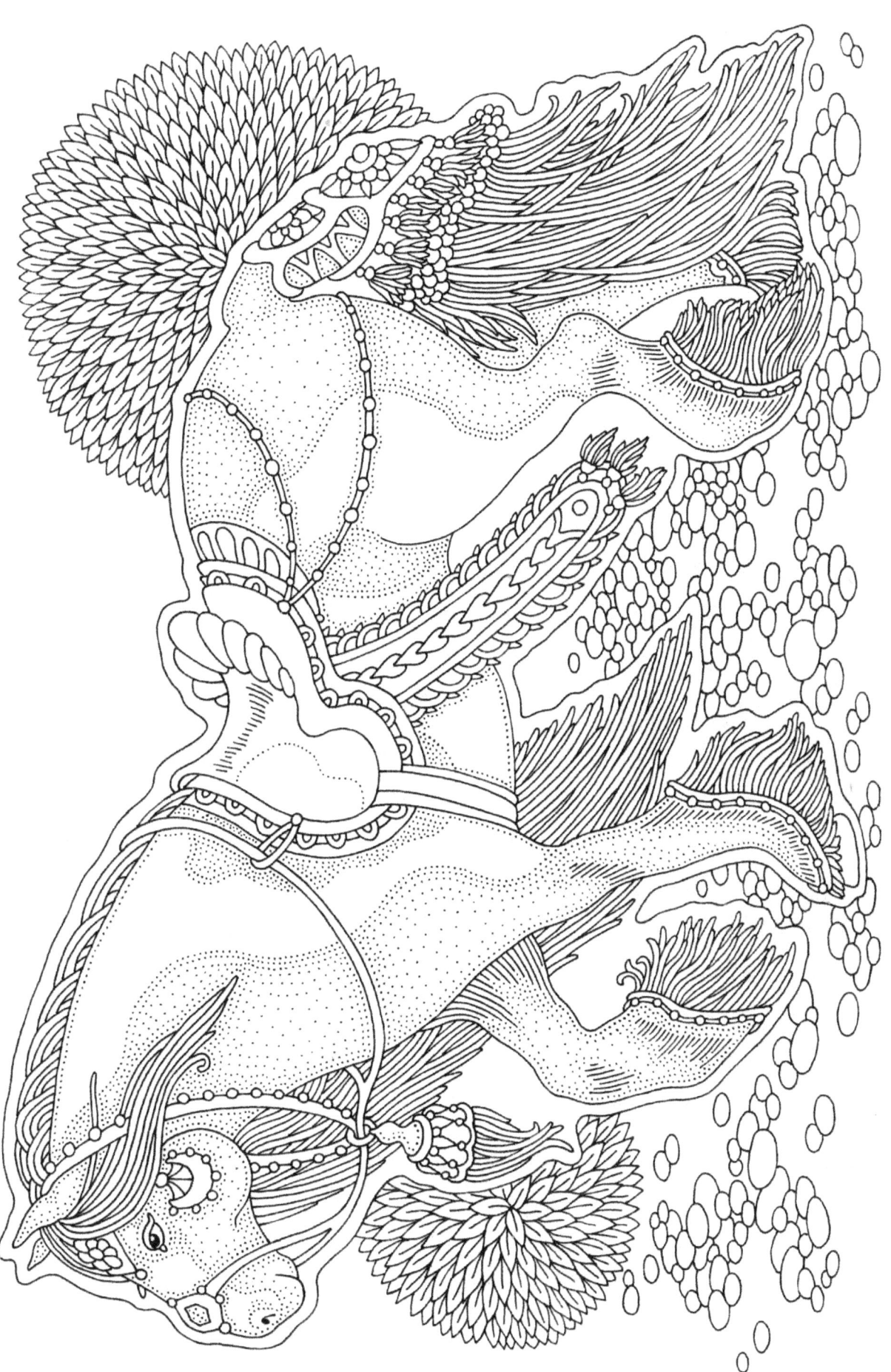

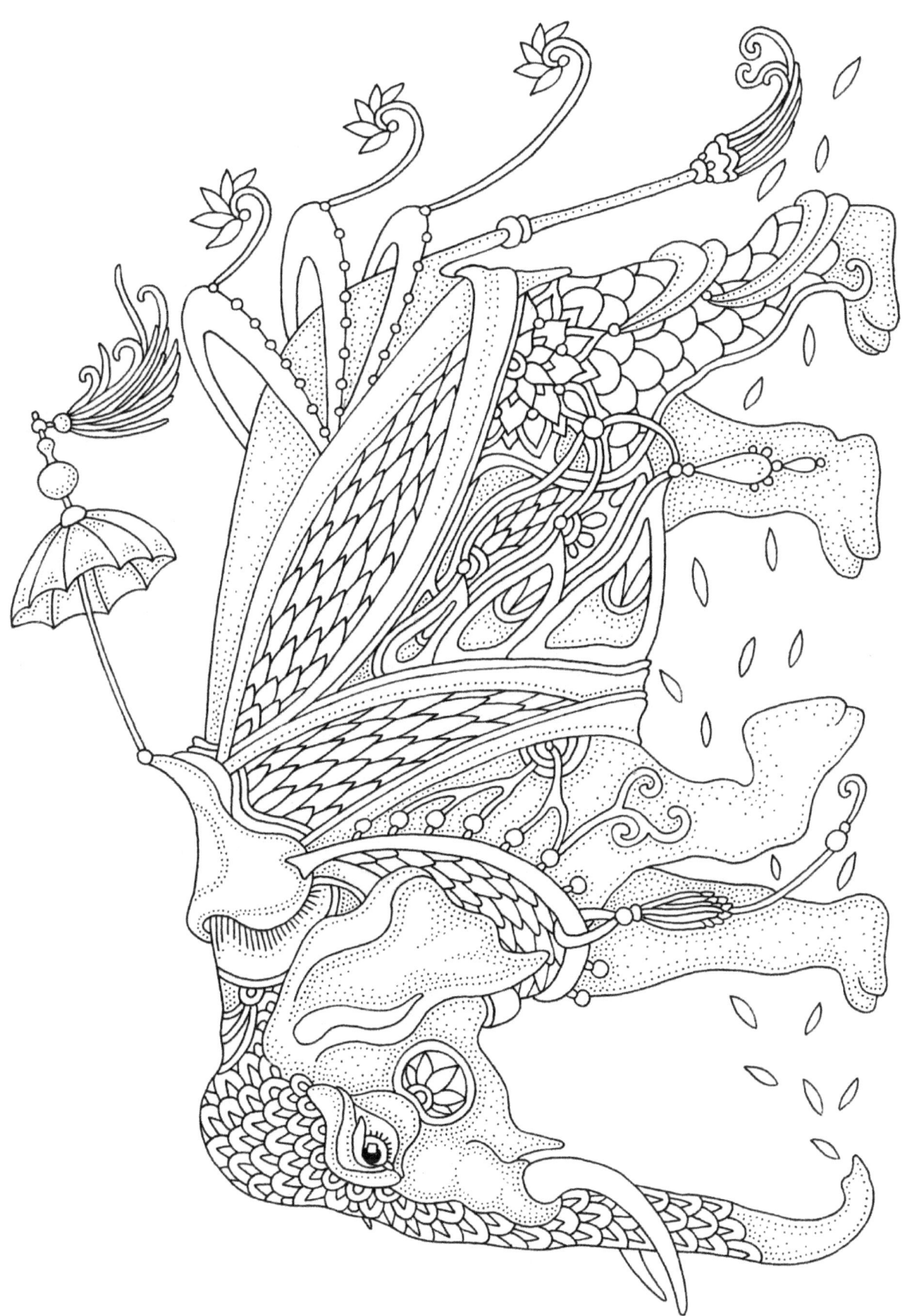

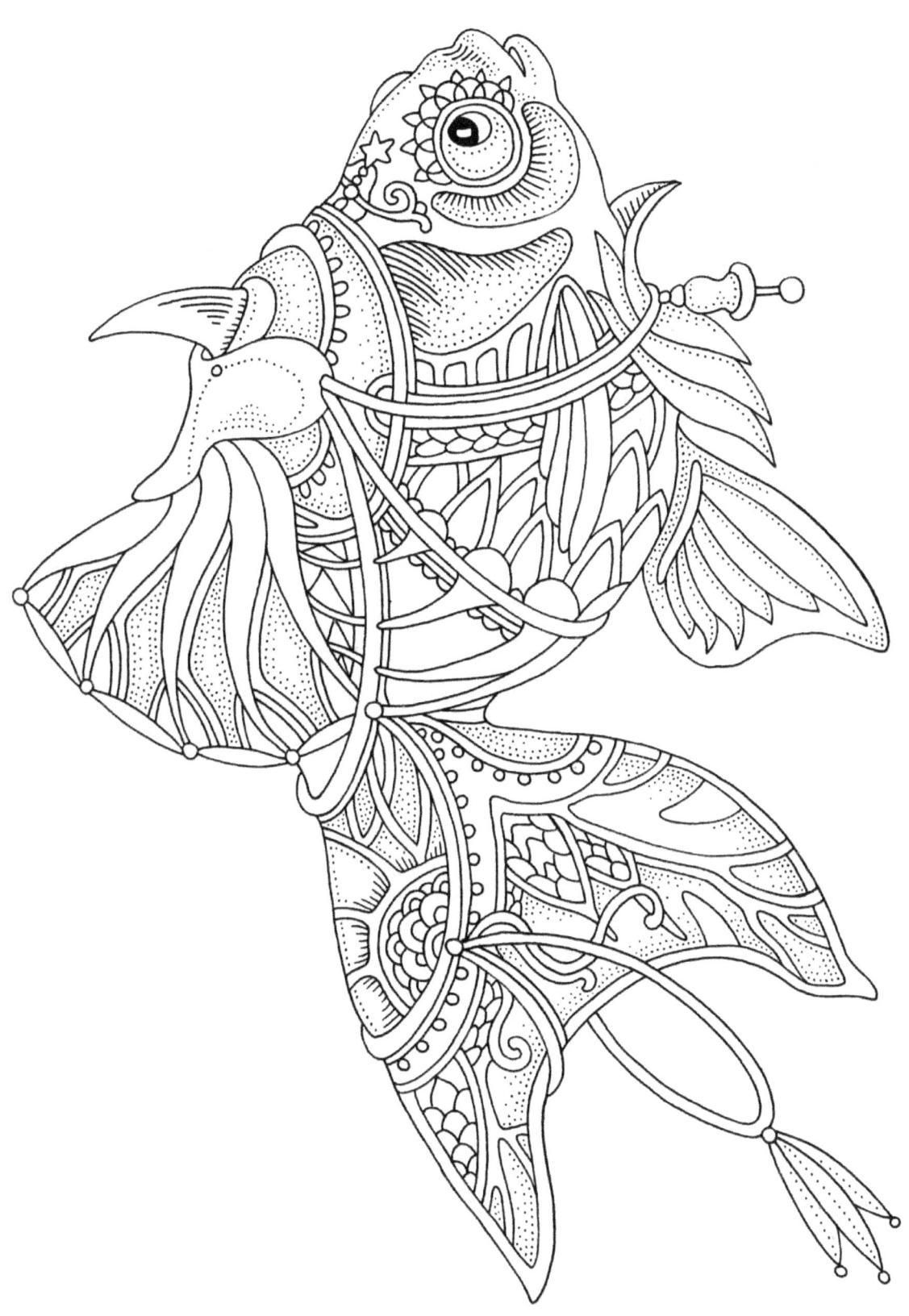

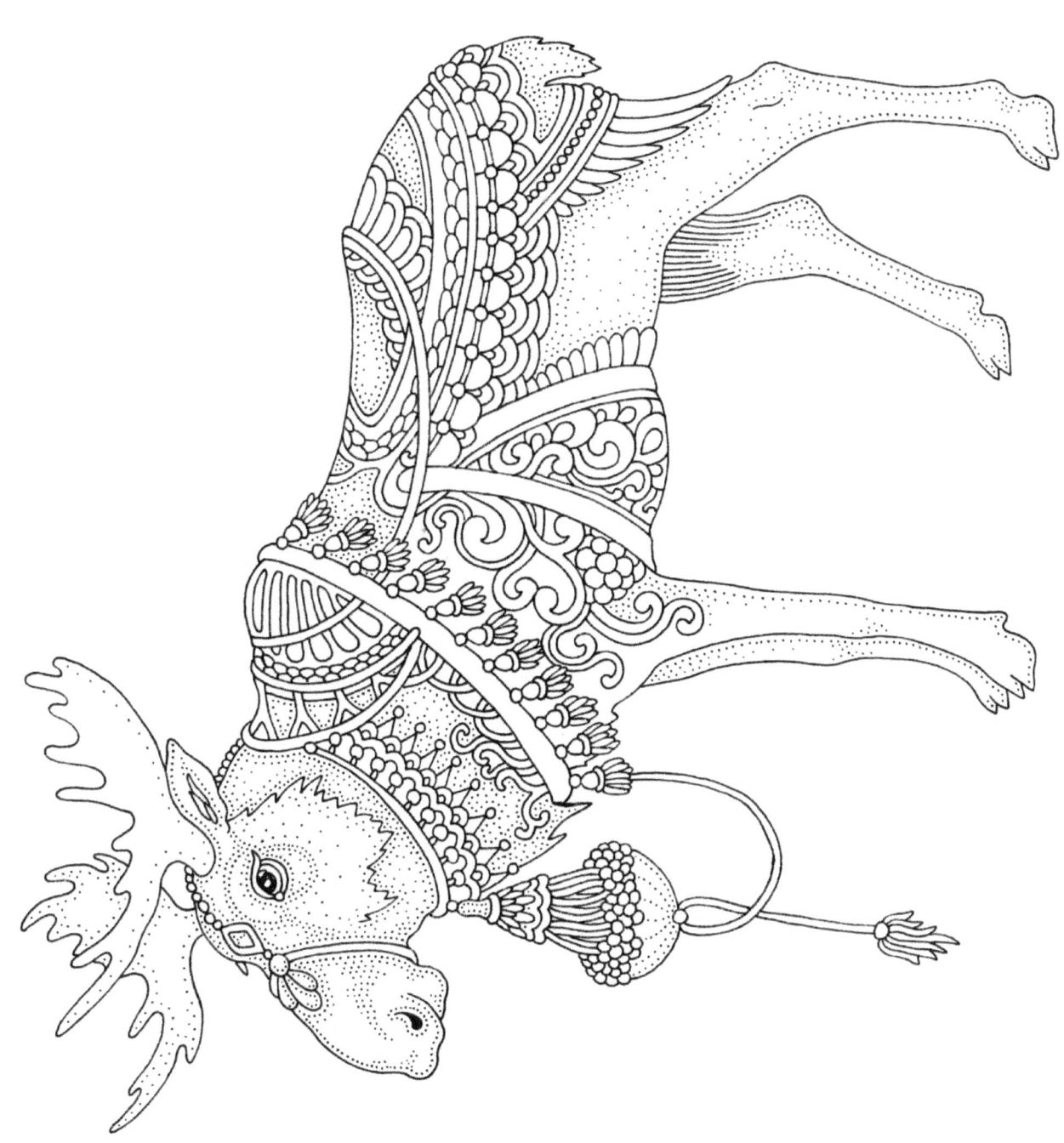

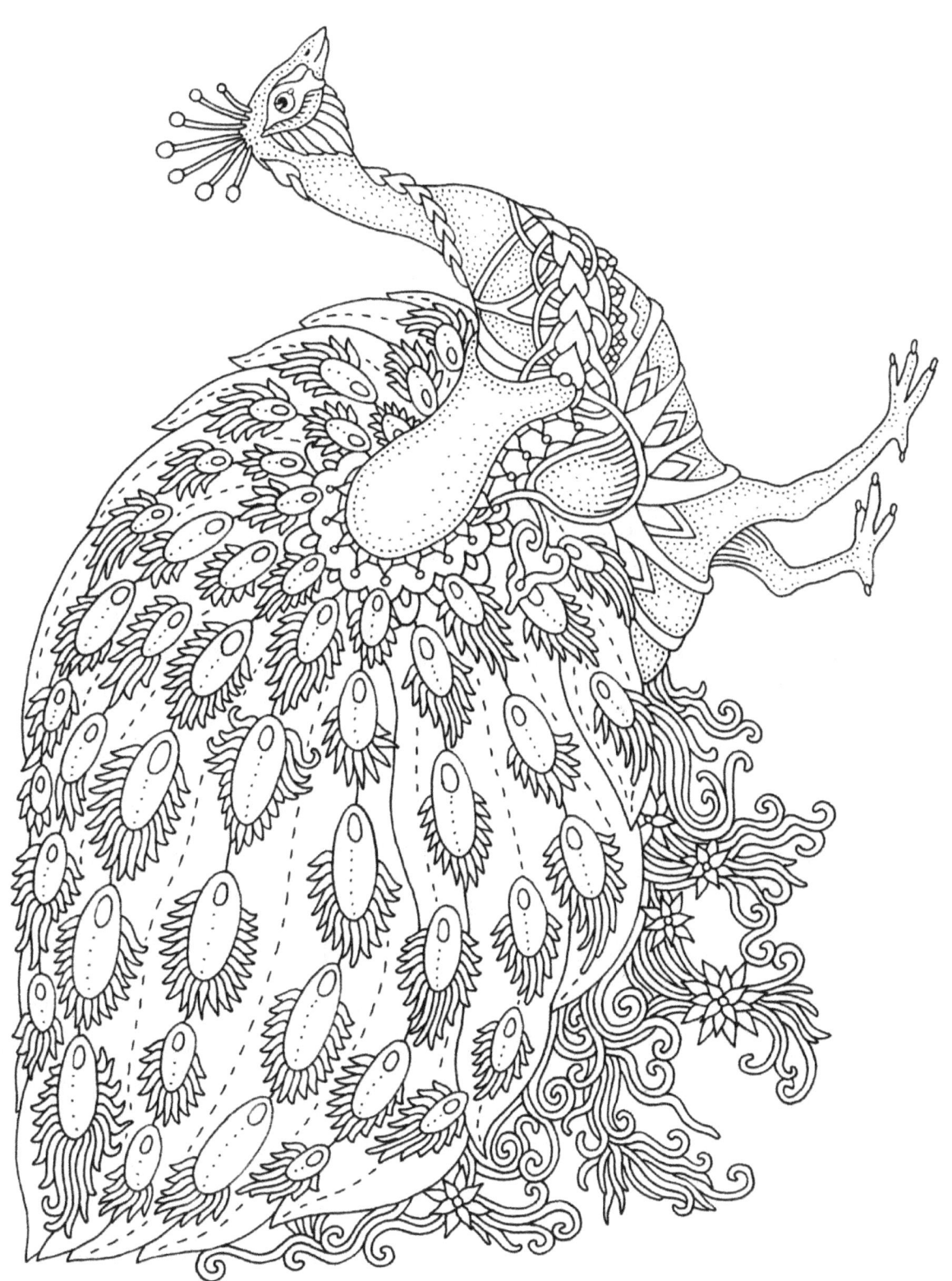

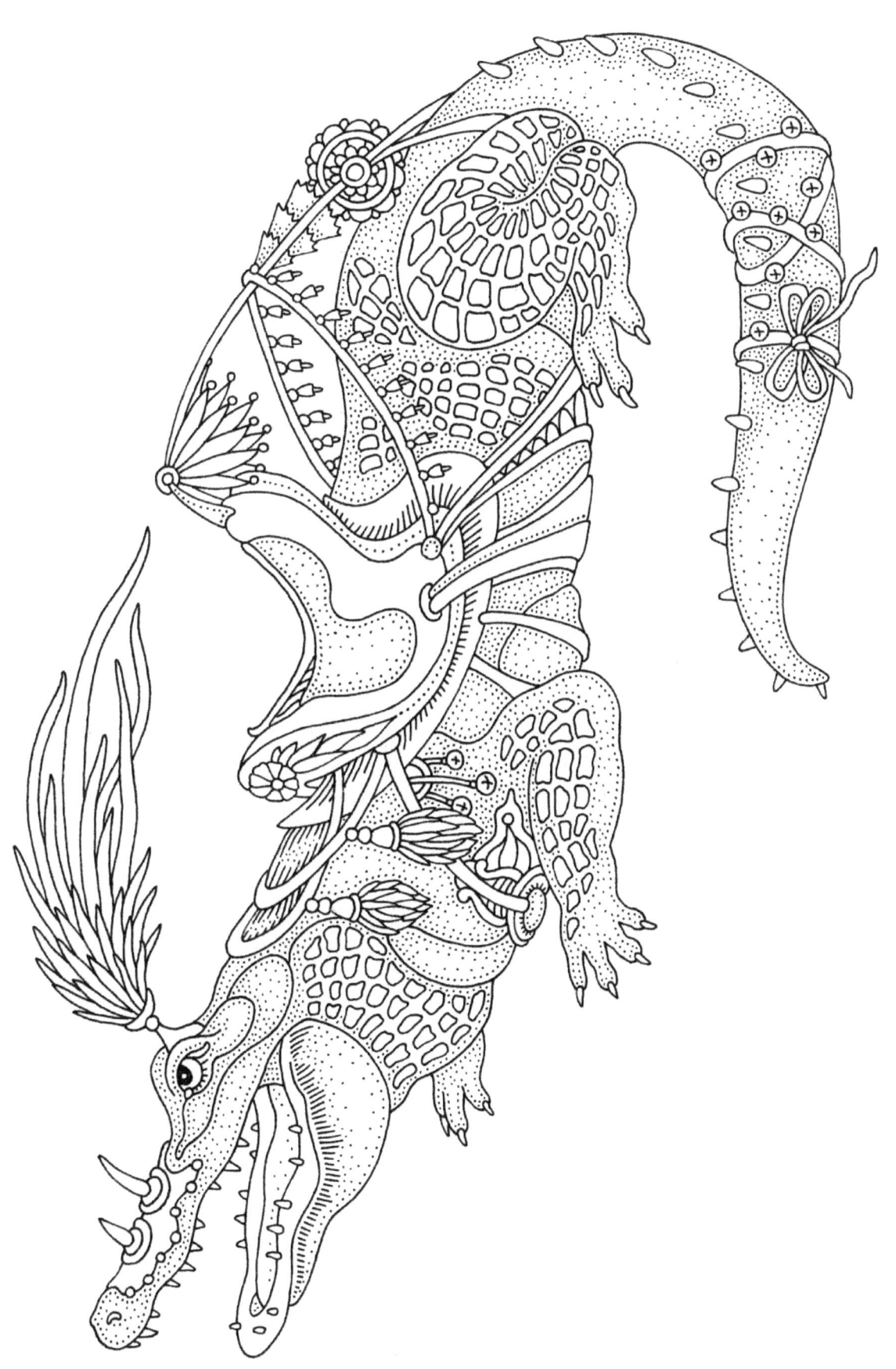

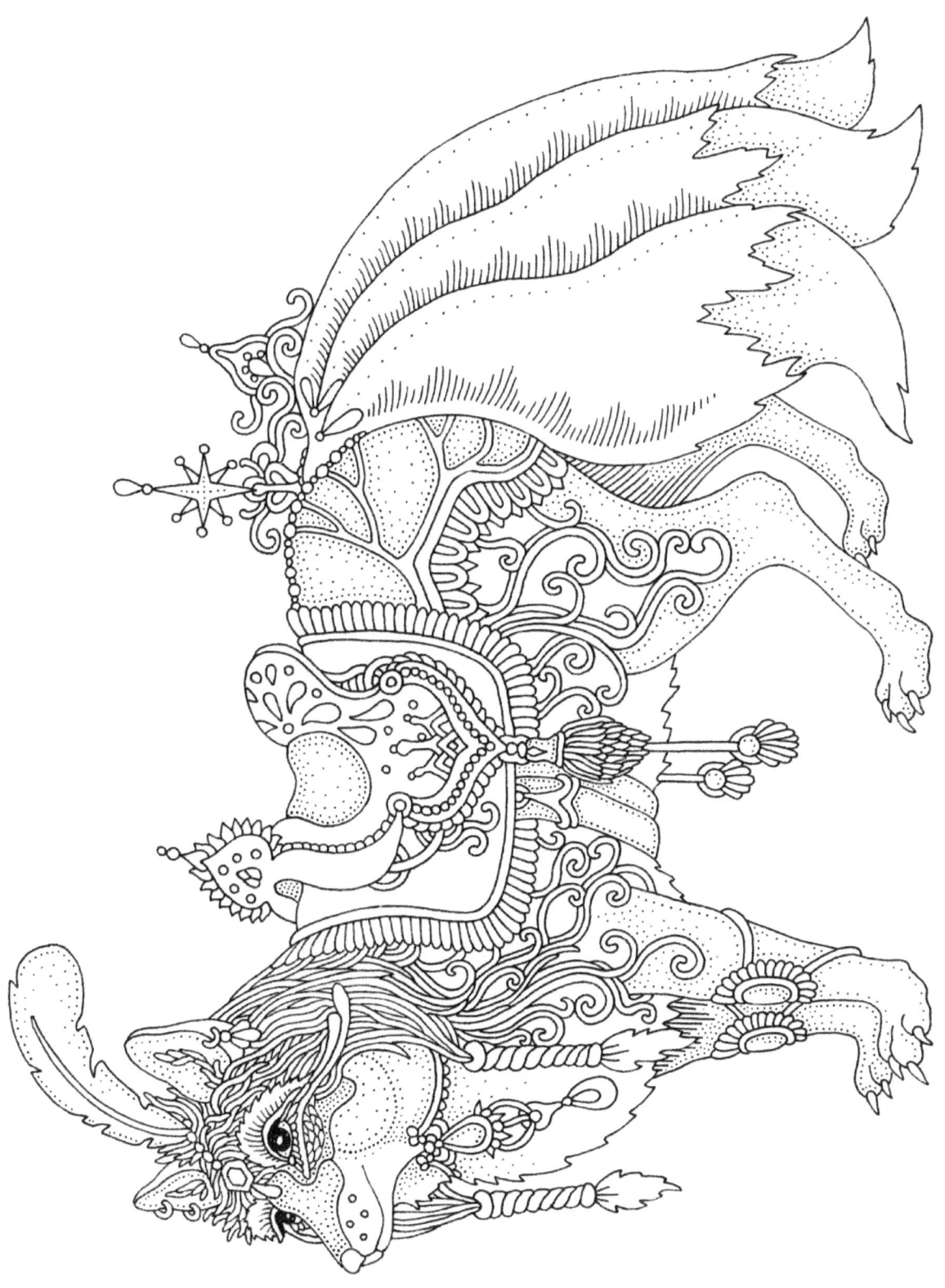

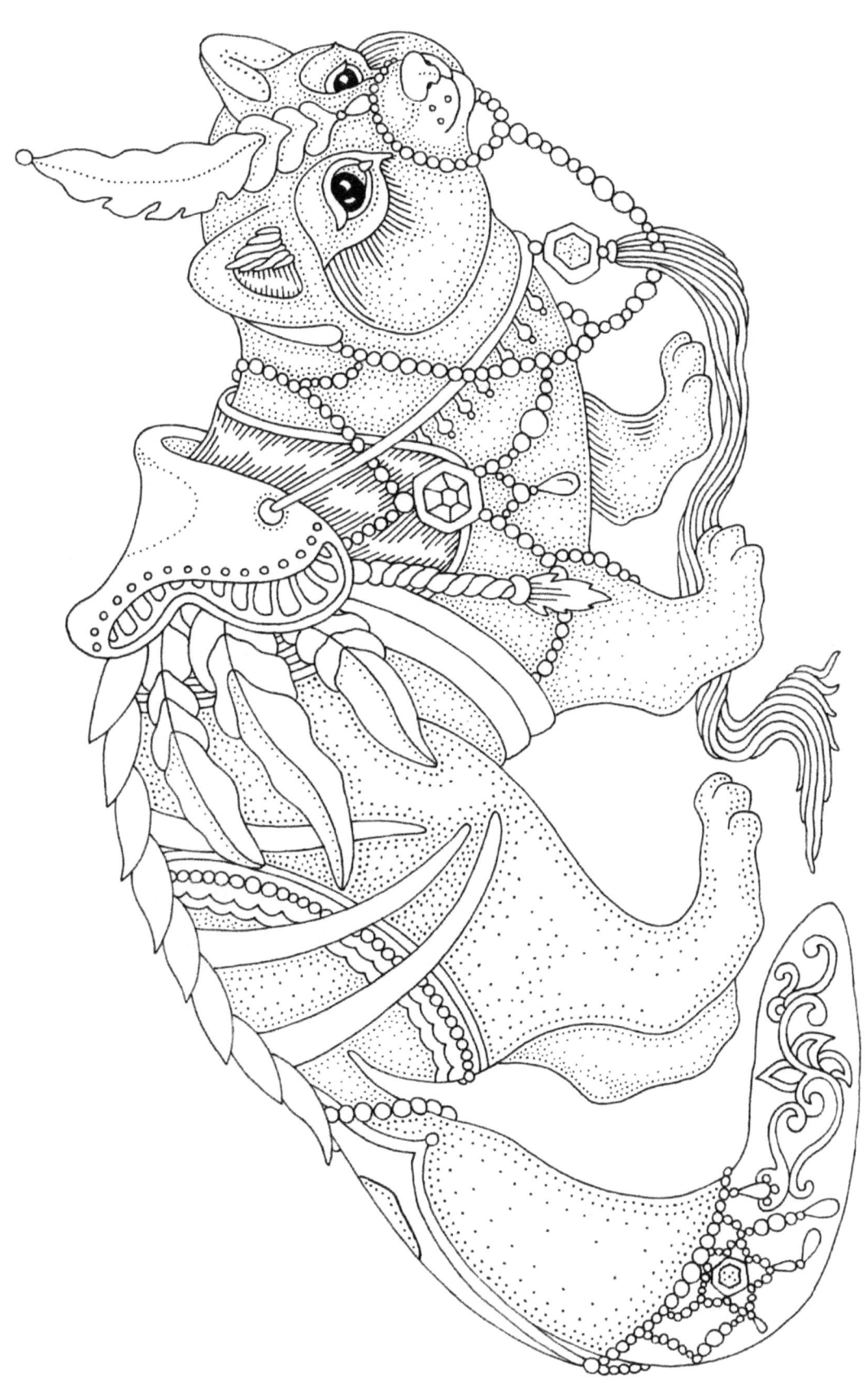

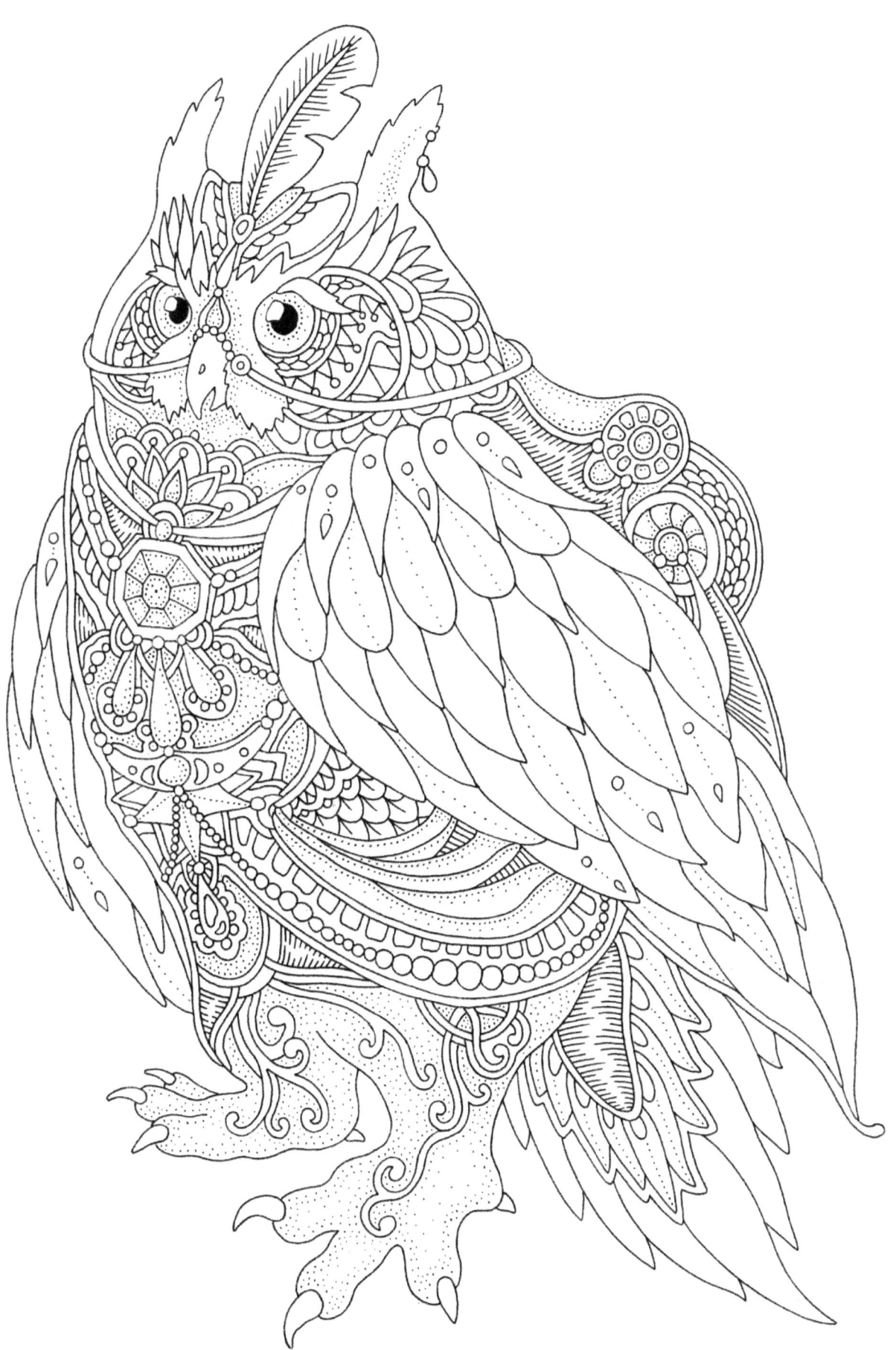

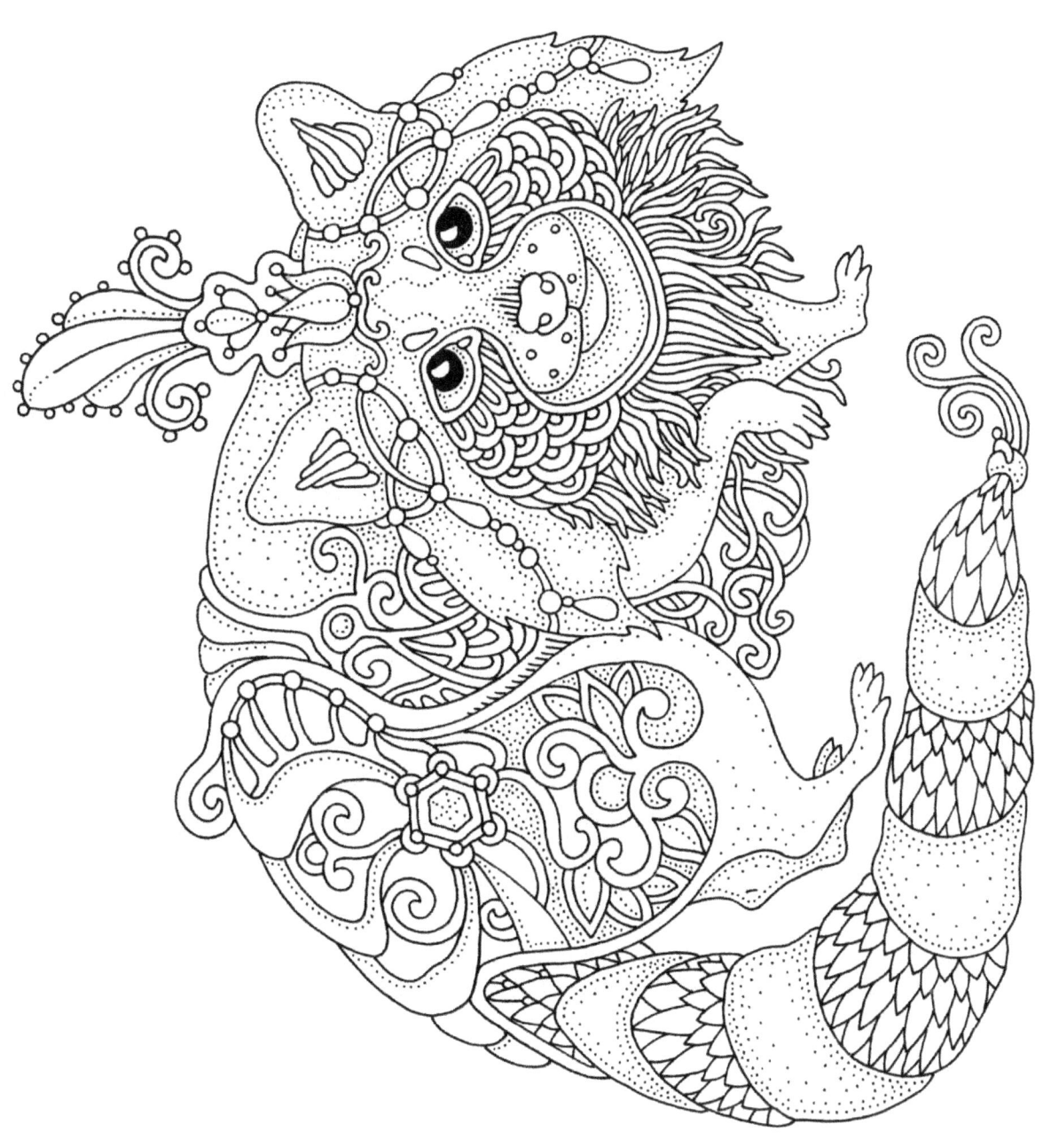

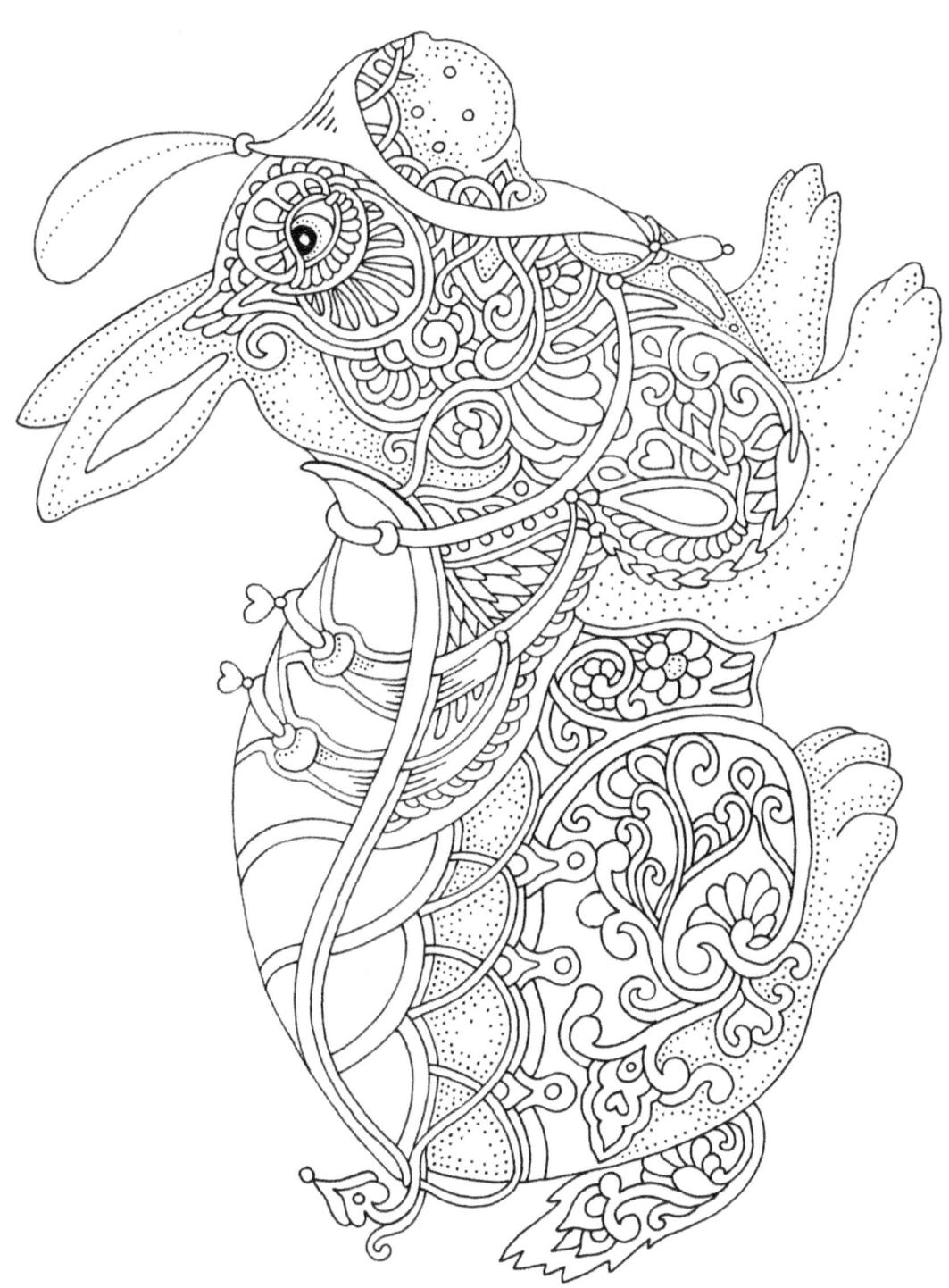

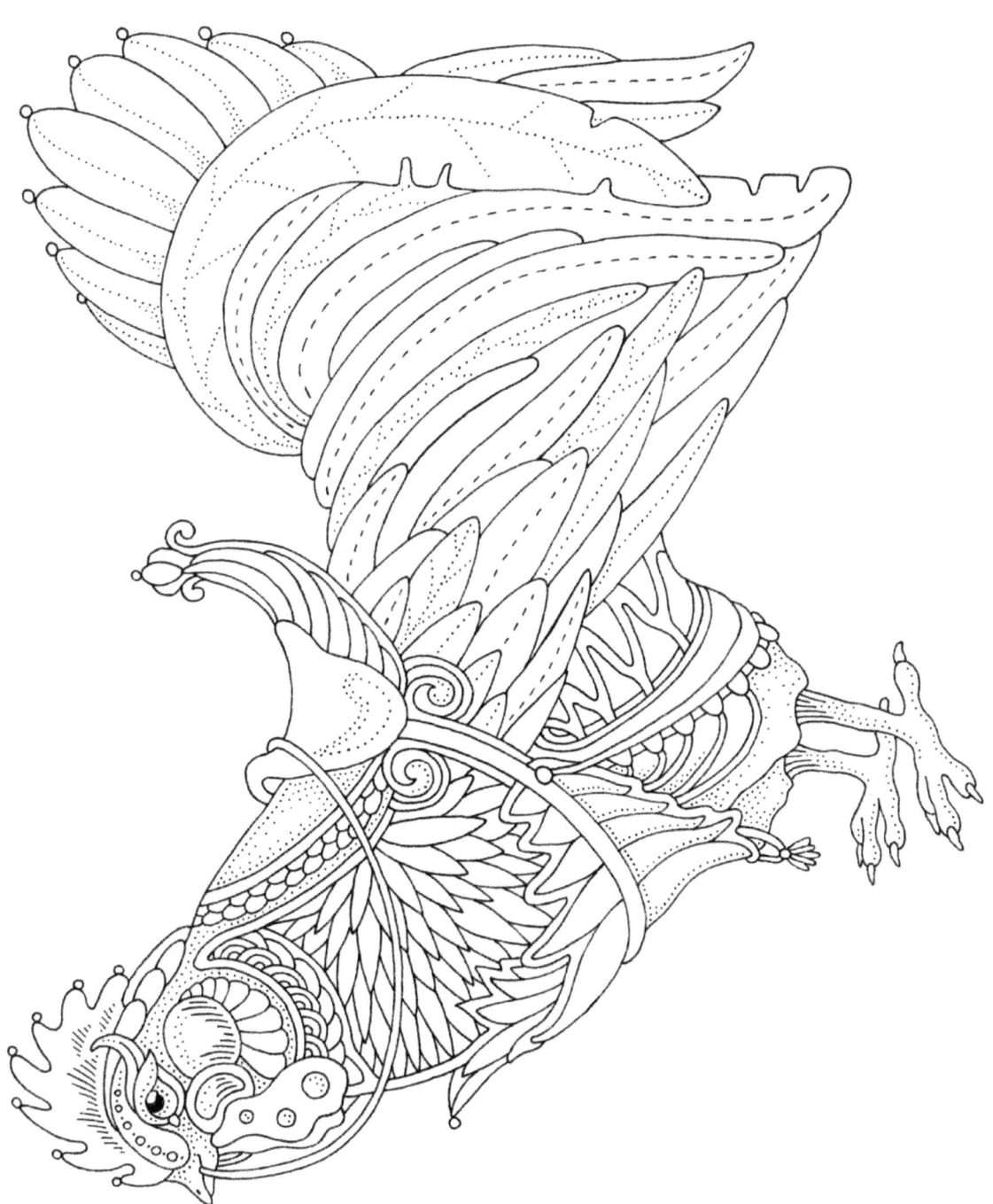

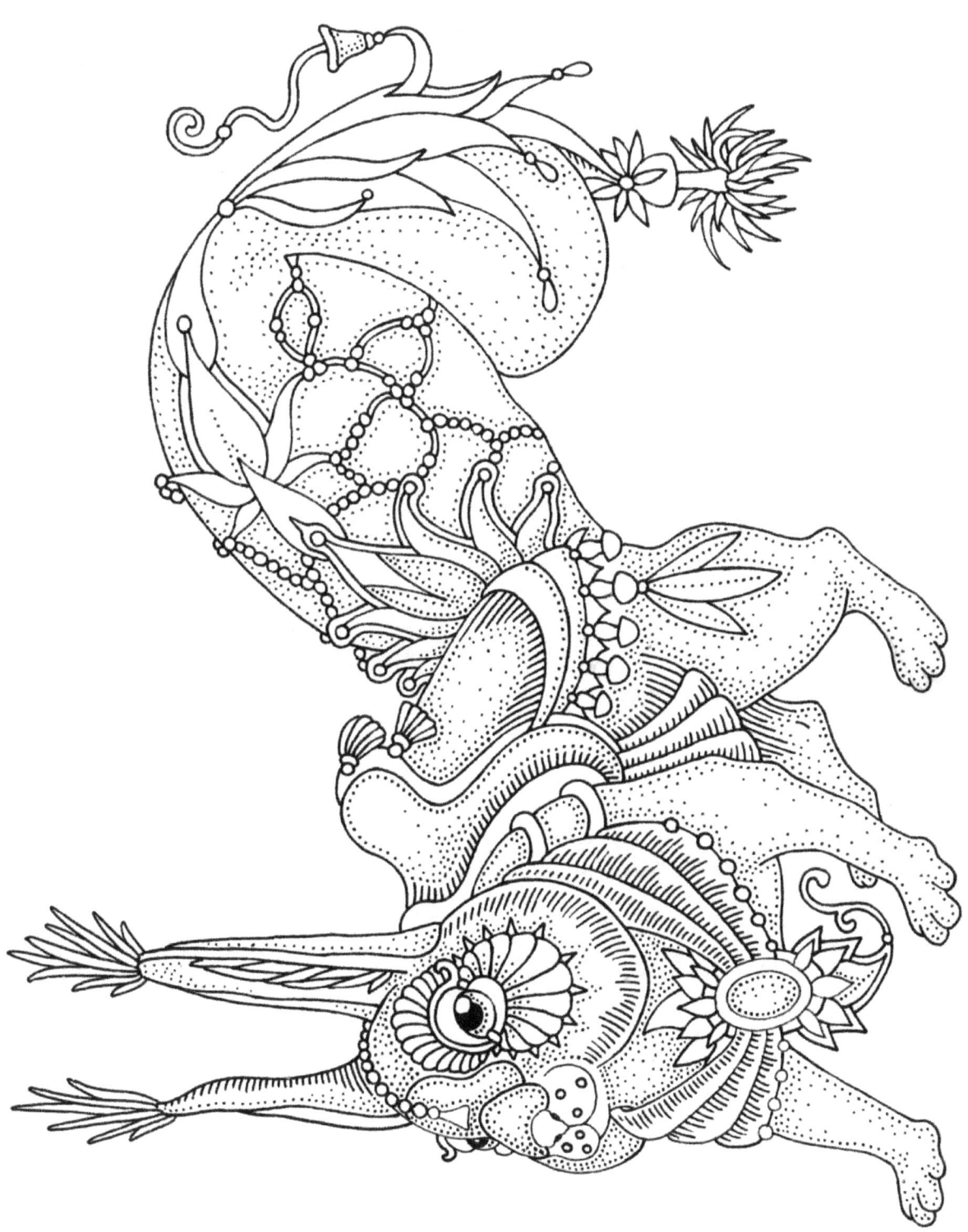

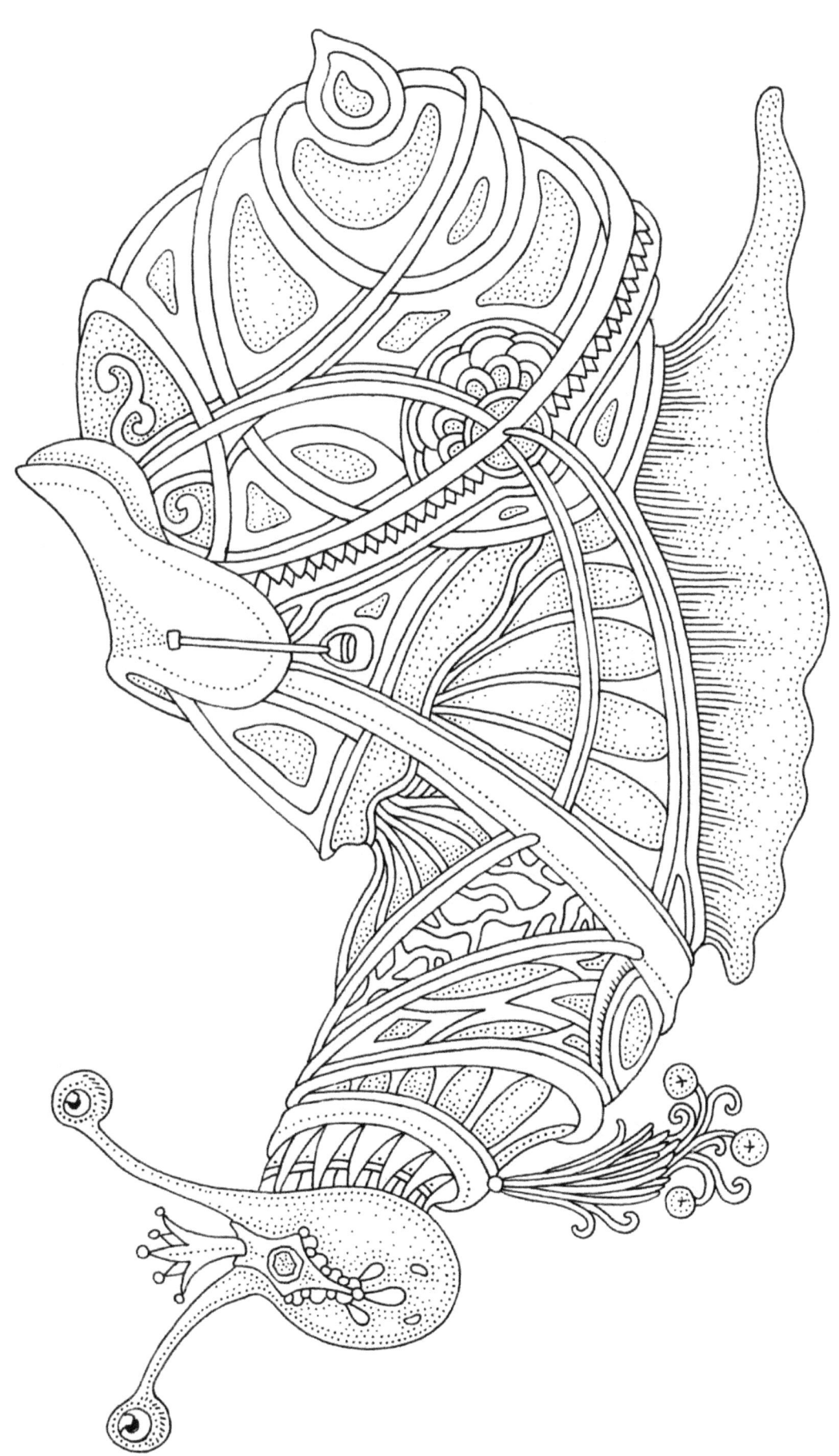

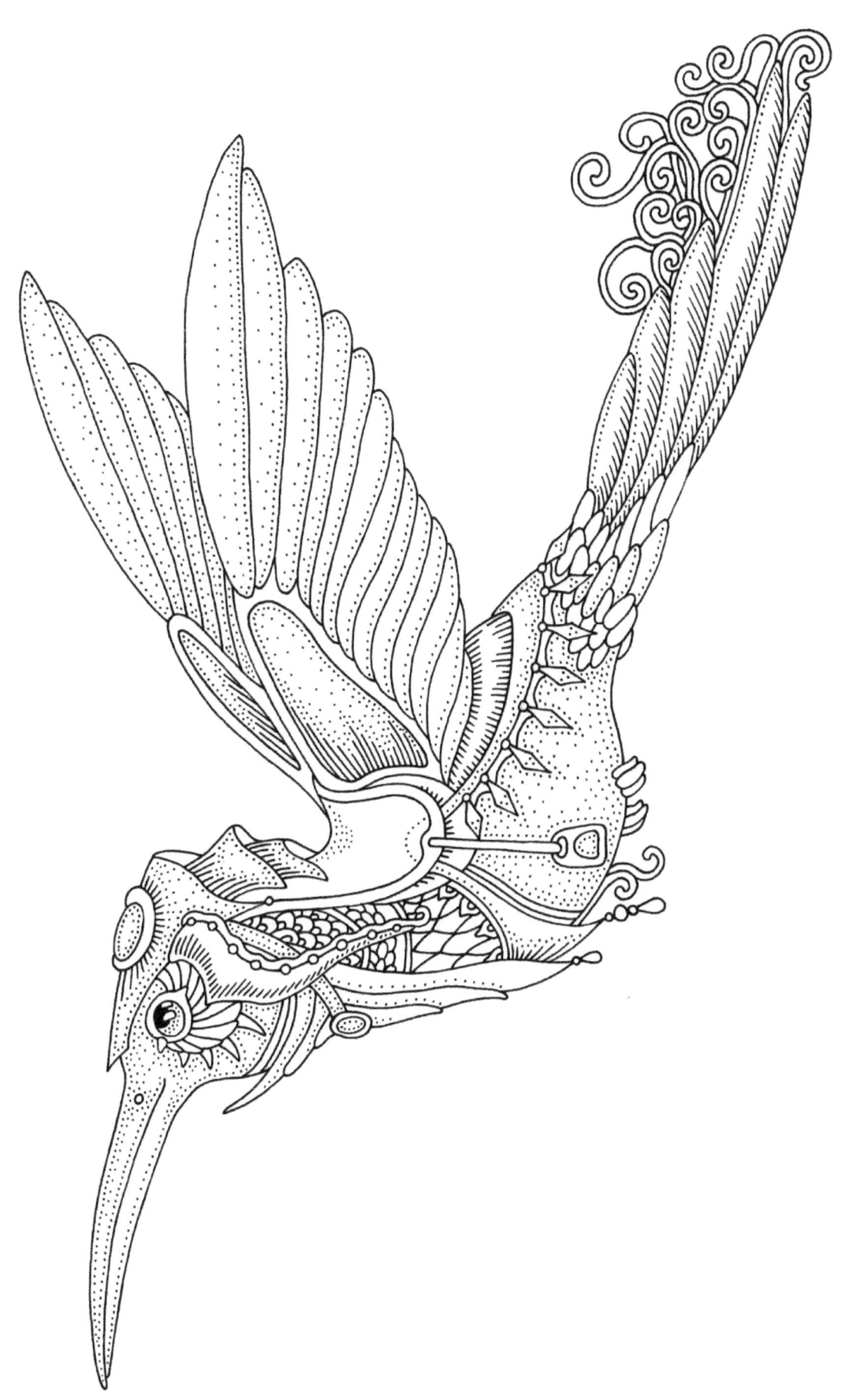

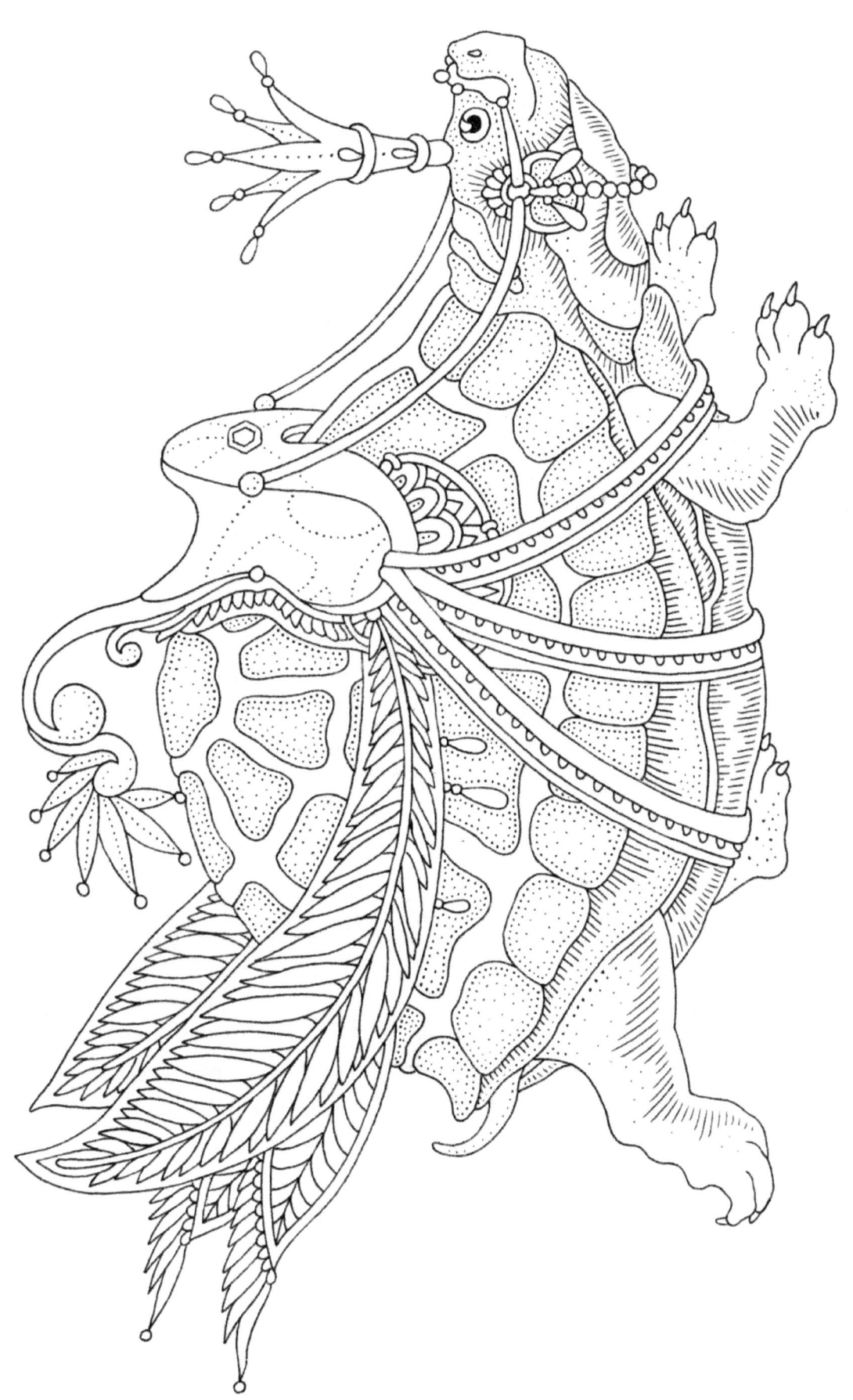

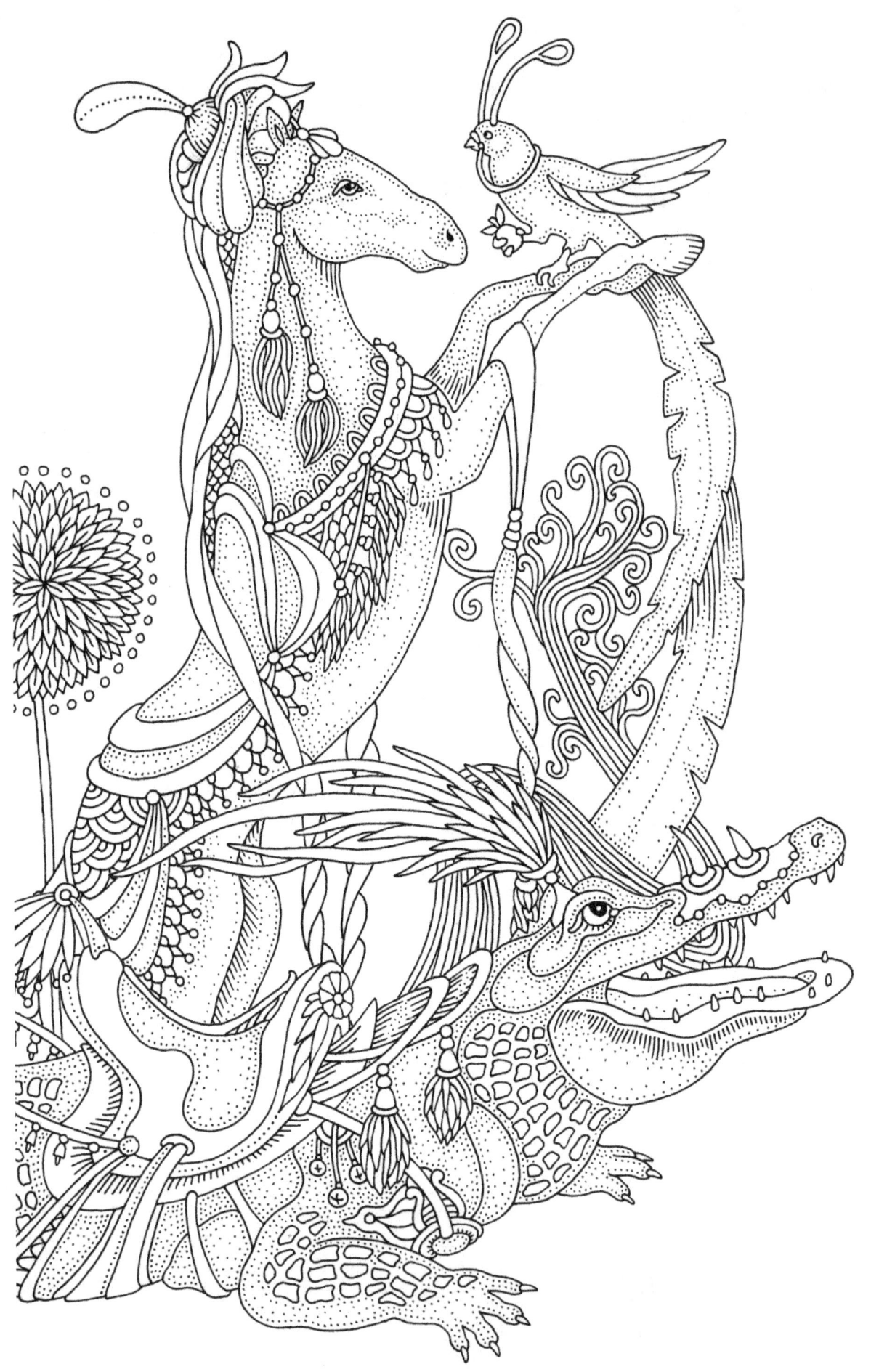

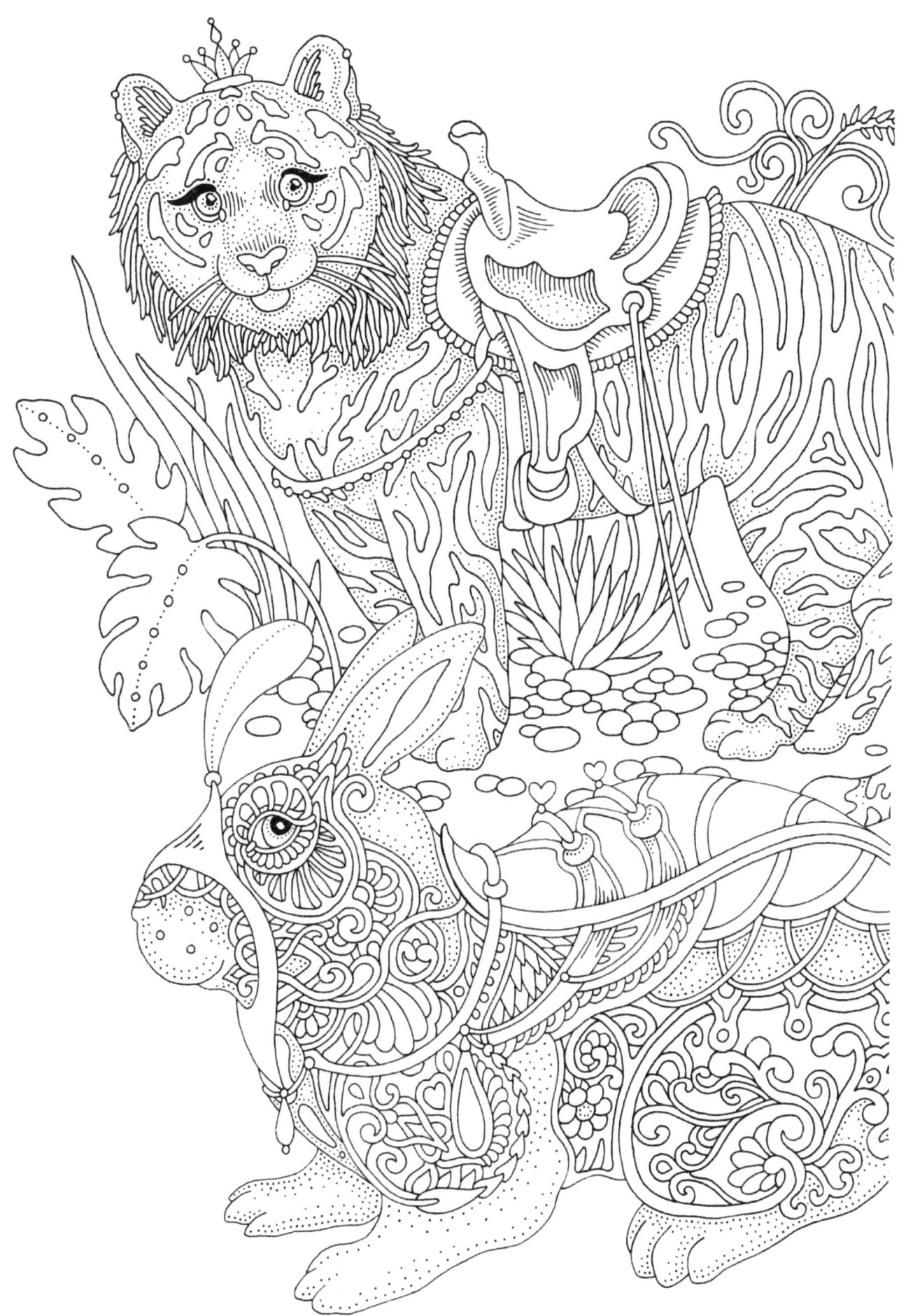